NEW Literacy Kit

Year 9

Geoff Barton

OXFORD
UNIVERSITY PRESS

OXFORD
UNIVERSITY PRESS

Great Clarendon Street, Oxford OX2 6DP

Oxford University Press is a department of the University of Oxford.
It furthers the University's objective of excellence in research, scholarship,
and education by publishing worldwide in

Oxford   New York

Auckland   Cape Town   Dar es Salaam   Hong Kong   Karachi
Kuala Lumpur   Madrid   Melbourne   Mexico City   Nairobi
New Delhi   Shanghai   Taipei   Toronto

With offices in

Argentina   Austria   Brazil   Chile   Czech Republic   France   Greece
Guatemala   Hungary   Italy   Japan   Poland   Portugal   Singapore
South Korea   Switzerland   Thailand   Turkey   Ukraine   Vietnam

Oxford is a registered trade mark of Oxford University Press
in the UK and in certain other countries

British Library Cataloguing in Publication Data

Data available

ISBN 978-0-19-832173-6

10 9 8

Printed by Vivar Printing Sdn Bhd., Malaysia

Assembled by Zed, Oxford.

ACKNOWLEDGEMENTS

The Publisher would like to thank the following for permission to reproduce
photographs:

p.8 OUP; **p.12** Topham Picturepoint; **p.14** PA Photos; **p.18** Adams Picture
Library; **p.19** Hemera/OUP; **p.20** OUP; **p.24** Adams Picture Library; **p.25**
Corel/OUP; **p.26** Alamy Images/Bill Bachman; **p.28** Adams Picture Library; **p.29**
Adams Picture Library; **p.30** Digital Vision/OUP; **p.31** Alamy Images/Kevin
Taylor; **p.32** OUP; **p.36** Waitrose Ltd; **p.37** Stockbyte/OUP; **p.39** OUP; **p.40**
Camera Press; **p.41** OUP; **p.42**(top) OUP; **p.42**(bottom) Mary Macnaghten/OUP;
p.47 Science Photo Library; **p.48** Science Photolibrary; **p.49** Science Photo
Library/Silkeborg Museum, Denmark; **p.50** Corbis/Jonathan Blair; **p.52** OUP;
p.55 Photostage/Donald Cooper; **p.56** Rex Features/Alex Oliveira; **p.57** Rex
Features/S Gaboury; **p.58** Photostage/Donald Cooper; **p.59** Robbie Jacks; **p.60**
OUP; **p.67** RSPCA/Andrew Forsyth; **p.68** Corel/OUP; **p.69** RSPCA/Cheryl A Ertelt;
p.71 Robert Harding World Imagery/Julia Rayne; **p.72** Corel/OUP; **p.73**
Photographers Library; **p.75** Photofusion/G Montgomery; **p.76** Alamy
Images/David Williams; **p.80** Robert Harding World Imagery; **p.83**
Photofusion/Paul Baldersare; **p.84** Alamy Images/David Hoffman; **p.86** OUP; **p.89**
John Birdsall Photo Library; **p.91** Corel/OUP; **p.92** Corel/OUP; **p.93** Superstock;
p.94 Photodisc/OUP; **p.97** Photonica/Christopher Wadsworth; **p.98** Corel/OUP;
p.99 Alamy Images/Pictor/RF; **p.100** Universal Pictorial Press; **p.101** Estate of
Janet Stone; **p.102** OUP; **p.108** OUP; **p.110** OUP/Michael Taylor; **p.111** OUP;
p.113 OUP; **p.117** OUP; **p.119** OUP; **p.120** OUP; **p.122** Mary Evans Picture
Library; **p.123** Mary Evans Picture Library; **p.126** Rex Features; **p.128**
Corel/OUP; **p.129** Photodisc/OUP; **p.130** OUP; **p.133** Mary Evans Picture Library;
p.135 OUP; **p.136** Alamy Images/Pixoi/RF; **p.137** OUP; Illustrated London
News/OUP; **p.140** OUP; **p.143** Movie Store; **p.147** Hemera/OUP; **p.148** OUP;
p.152 Corel/OUP; **p.155** Bridgeman Art Library; **p.157** OUP.

Illustrations are by Martin Aston **p.115**; Andy Hammond **p.15**; Peter Melnyczuk
p.124, **p.125**; Richard Morris **p.114**.

Cartoon icons are by David Semple.

Cover photograph: Mark Mason/OUP

Crown Copyright material: extracts from 'Sun Know-how' from www.doh.gov.uk
and 'Sun Safety' from www.wiredforhealth.gov.uk are reproduced under Class
Licence Number C01P0000148 with the permission of the Controller of HMSO
and the Queen's Printer for Scotland.

We are also grateful for permission to reprint from the following:

Michael Asher: extract from *A Desert Dies* (Viking, 1986), reprinted by permission
of David Higham Associates.

Steve Callahan: extract from *Adrift* (Bantam, 1986) reprinted by permission of
Abner Stein.

Frances Cornford: 'A Recollection'' from *Collected Poems* (Cresset Press,
1954eprinted by permission of the Trustees of the Mrs Frances Cornford
Deceased Will Trust c/o Barr Ellison Solicitors.

Len Deighton: extract from 'Mission Control: Cannibal One' in *Declarations of War*
(Jonathan Clowes, 1971), copyright © Len Deighton 1971, © 2001 Pluriform
Publishing Company BV, reprinted by permission of Jonathan Clowes Ltd,
London, on behalf of Pluriform Publishing Company BV.

Emily Dickinson: 'There's Been a Death' from *The Poems of Emily Dickinson*, edited
by Thomas H Johnson, (The Belknap Press of Harvard University Press),
copyright © 1951, 1955, 1979 by the President and Fellows of Harvard College,
reprinted by permission of the publishers and Trustees of Amherst College.

Seamus Heaney: 'Mid-Term Break' from *Death of a Naturalist* (1966), reprinted by
permission of the publishers, Faber & Faber Ltd.

Ian Herbert: 'In a Lancashire village, a cat a day is vanishing into thin air. What
is going on?', *The Independent*, 20.11.99, copyright © The Independent 1999,
reprinted by permission of The Independent.

Andy Martin: extract from *Walking on Water* (John Murray, 1995), reprinted by
permission of David Higham Associates.

Michael Meyer (translator): extract from Henrik Ibsen: *An Enemy of the People*
(Methuen, 1974), reprinted by permission of the publisher.

Arthur Miller (translator): extract from Henrik Ibsen: *An Enemy of the People* (Nick
Hern Books, 1989), copyright © 1950, 1951, 1989 by Arthur Miller, reprinted by
permission of the publishers: www.nickhernbooks.co.uk

Bill Mouland and Stephen Wright: 'An Ealing Comedy of Errors', *Daily Mail*,
8.11.00, reprinted by permission of Solo Syndication Ltd.

Stevie Smith: 'Not Waving but Drowning' from *Collected Poems of Stevie Smith*
(Penguin Modern Classics), copyright © 1972 Stevie Smith, reprinted by
permission of The Executors of James MacGibbon.

We thank the following for permission to reproduce copyright material:

Abbot Mead Vickers BBDO Ltd and the RSPCA for script of 'Swim' radio
advertisement.

Friends of the Earth for extract from www.foe.co.uk web site.

Private Eye (Pressdram Ltd) for 'The Glamis Herald', *Private Eye*, issue 843, 8.4.94

The Vegetarian Society for extracts from their web site www.vegsoc.org.

Waitrose/John Lewis Partnership for extracts from leaflet 'Why we need meat,
poultry and fish'.

Short extracts on pages 105–106 are reproduced from:
A. Tom Wolfe: *The Purple Decades* (Jonathan Cape, 1983)
B. Antonia White: 'A Child of the Five Woods'
C. Robert Fisk: *Pity the Nation* (Andre Deutsch, 1990)
D. Bella Bathurst: *The Lighthouse Stevensons* (HarperCollins, 1999)
E. Sebastian Faulks: *Birdsong* (Hutchinson, 1993)

We have tried to trace and contact all copyright holders before publication. If
notified, the publishers will be pleased to rectify any errors or omissions at the
earliest opportunity.

Paper used in the production of this book is a natural, recyclable product made
from wood grown in sustainable forests. The manufacturing process conforms to
the environmental regulations of the country of origin.

Contents

Introduction

New Literacy Kit has been written to build your skills in English, develop your self-confidence, and make you an expert in working with a range of different texts. This new edition provides starters, texts, activities and assessment tasks which will help you to see what you are doing well and what you need to work on.

The Year 9 Students' Book combines texts from the three writing triplets:

- ◆ Inform, Explain, Describe
- ◆ Persuade and Analyse
- ◆ Imagine, Explore, Entertain

These are based on the national curriculum for English (though we have linked 'persuade' and 'analyse' together to build your understanding of them). By grouping texts like this, you will be able to develop a deeper understanding of the way different text types work. This is essential preparation for helping you to write in a range of styles and across your different subjects at school.

As always in English, these categories will often overlap, but knowing that you are covering all parts of the English curriculum will help to build your confidence.

This is how each unit is organized:

Getting started

Each unit has a starter activity. Starters are great fun because they get your brain working. They lead you into a topic with lively, often unexpected tasks, which tend to involve minimum writing and maximum thinking. Use these activities to loosen your brain up, practise your teamwork, and feel your way into the main topic of the unit.

Learning objectives

The learning objectives help to map out the learning journey ahead of you. They don't tell you what you will do but what you will learn. That's really important – having a clear sense from the beginning of what you are expected to learn.

Introduction

This briefly sets the scene for each text, tuning you into the context of the material and helping you to know when it was written, by whom, and for what purpose. The more we know about texts in advance, the better prepared we are for discussing, understanding and exploring them. In this section, you may be asked to think about questions or ideas before reading the texts, or to make predictions about what might happen in them.

To do well in English, you need to have an understanding of why you are reading a text and how it relates to other texts you know. The introductions are designed to help you build this understanding.

Texts and activities

The texts have been carefully selected to interest and entertain you, and to help develop your knowledge of different text types. They are followed by questions, tasks and activities which are grouped in three ways:

- First, there are questions about understanding the text. These should build your confidence quickly by allowing you to spot key features and to show that you understand what the text is about.

- Next, you are asked questions about interpreting the text. These questions are more open-ended. They give you a chance to explore your own responses and to give your own opinions.

- Finally, there is a section on language and structure, which is a key part of your work in English. The work you do with language and structure will help you to become familiar with the language choices that writers make, and allow you to explore details at word, sentence and text level.

Writing activity

You can develop your understanding of the text further in the writing activity. It encourages you to see things from the point of view of the writer – testing out ideas, writing creatively and reflecting on your own language decisions.

Extended writing

Each unit gives you an opportunity to put into practice the skills you have learned earlier on. You'll be able to practise structuring your ideas, linking words and sentences, choosing the right vocabulary and making the right impact on your reader. The extended writing task always builds on the skills you have covered in the unit, so you should feel a real sense of making progress.

Assess your learning

This section helps you to review your own progress – not through formal tests and exams, but by helping you to evaluate your development against the learning objectives of the unit.

Speaking and listening

To make progress in English, speaking and listening is an essential lesson ingredient. In *New Literacy Kit*, listening and speaking are built in, from starter activities to assessment. In the process you should develop a better understanding of your own skills and qualities in speaking and as a listener.

Above all, *New Literacy Kit* has been designed as a lively and thought-provoking resource that helps you to make real progress in English. I hope you enjoy using it.

Geoff Barton

Inform, Explain, Describe

Getting started
Unit 1 Media recounts

Newspaper recounts usually give a lot of information in relatively few words. Headlines are often shortened sentences, and can be ambiguous (have more than one meaning). Read the headlines below.

> Salesmen will hear car talk at noon

> School bus passengers should be belted, say safety experts

> Police begin campaign to run down jaywalkers

a Explain how these headlines are ambiguous.

b Do you think ambiguity can have a positive effect? If so, how?

c What do you think makes a good headline? (Think about its main purpose and how it can achieve it.)

Unit 2 Travel writing

Travel writing often uses descriptive language to bring people and places to life. Good travel writing makes the reader feel what it is actually like to be in a particular place at a particular time.

Take the room you are currently in. Work with a partner to think of the best descriptive sentence to capture the atmosphere of the room. Avoid starting 'The room is …' Instead, choose a particular detail to describe, for example, 'Faces beam down from posters on high walls …'

Share your descriptions with the rest of the class and decide which is the most interesting and evocative.

Unit 3 Information texts to persuade

Some information texts use facts and statistics to try to persuade their audience to a certain viewpoint or action.

With a partner, choose one of the topics below:

- Exercise is a good thing
- Watching too much TV isn't a good thing
- The Internet can be unsafe for young children

Decide what facts and statistics you would include if you were to write an information text about the topic. List the facts and statistics that you already know as well as those that you would research.

Unit 4 Explanations

Many lessons in school aim to explain things, such as scientific concepts, geographical processes or ICT procedures. Think of all the handouts and worksheets you are given by teachers to explain concepts, processes and ideas.

From your experience:

◆ Which three ingredients are generally in the best handouts?

◆ Which three ingredients are generally in the worst handouts?

With a partner, draw up a checklist of features that you would advise teachers to use in their explanation handouts. You might wish to include visuals in your list, as well as words.

Unit 5 Playing with non-fiction conventions

A parody mimics the style of something else, for comic effect. Work in pairs or triplets to parody a news report, using role play.

1 First, choose a well-known nursery rhyme with some dramatic action in it (e.g. 'Humpty Dumpty').

2 Then, decide who will be the news presenter (anchor person); who will be the reporter at the scene; and who will be an eyewitness being interviewed.

3 Next, decide roughly what each person will say (there is no need to script word for word).

4 Finally, play your parts, using Standard English. The secret of parody is to do it as seriously as possible.

You could use opening phrases such as:

◆ *And the headlines this evening …*

◆ *Now some breaking news, and we head across to our reporter …*

◆ *Nick, I'm speaking to you from …*

◆ *We believe Mr Dumpty is in a stable but critical condition …*

What is a media recount?

Introduction

Recounts tell us about past events. They may include autobiography, newspaper articles, reports and historical texts. Most recounts:

♦ aim to inform and entertain

♦ are structured in **chronological order**

♦ use the **first person** (autobiography) or the **third person** (history)

♦ aim to paint pictures in words, so they may use plenty of **description**.

Newspaper recounts

This unit focuses on the types of recounts found in the media, and how they use description.

Newspapers use their front page to inform readers about the stories that seem most important. They then sometimes include further articles on the same topic later in the newspaper, or on a later date. Here the purpose might be to provide more detailed information or different viewpoints. Our first extract is of this type.

Newspapers also investigate events that are not major news – mysteries, amusing stories, or local events. The second extract in this unit is an example of this type of article.

News article

An Ealing Comedy of Errors

Learning objectives

This extract gives newspaper readers the facts about a news event. These are the objectives you will be studying:

- Word level: recognize layers of meaning

- Sentence level: vary the formality of your writing; integrate speech, reference and quotation into your writing; develop your paragraphing skills

- Reading: evaluate print, ICT and media texts; explore how media texts influence their readers; analyse the author's standpoint; explore the use of rhetorical devices

- Writing: explore how information texts can be entertaining; use descriptive detail

Introduction

This extract gives the 'inside story' about a daring raid at the Millennium Dome in Greenwich, on 7 November 2000. The main story was printed on pages 1 and 2 of the *Daily Mail*. Inside the newspaper this article was printed. It aims to give more detailed information, using language and images to help explain what happened.

Glossary

Ealing comedy – *early British comedy films which were made at studios in Ealing*

The Sweeney – *violent 1970s television series*

audacious – *recklessly daring*

AN EALING COMEDY OF ERRORS

By Bill Mouland and Stephen Wright

After months of meticulous planning, the raiders must have thought nothing could stop them

A boat was waiting to whisk the gang away. So were the police.

It was like a scene from 'The Sweeney' as the gang's stolen JCB smashed into the Dome and roared towards its multi-million target.

With a speedboat idling its powerful engines on the Thames outside and a lookout monitoring police radio frequencies on the opposite bank, the thieves must have thought nothing could stop them.

But a gritty drama of criminal daring swiftly turned into something more akin to an Ealing comedy. For police had known about the plot for two months and 100 officers were lying in wait – some disguised as cleaners, others as tourists.

Staff from De Beers, which owns the Millennium Star and the other 11 rare blue diamonds in the spectacular Money Zone display, were also in on the act and had already swapped the real gems for fakes.

The police watched and waited as four of the gang, all wearing gas masks and bulletproof vests, let off smoke bombs and thunder flashes in the vault.

They were starting to attack the display with nail guns and sledgehammers when the Flying Squad, the real-life Sweeney, went into action.

Shouting, 'Stop! Armed police,' about 20 officers surrounded the gang while snipers held them in their sights from overhead gantries.

They gave up without a fight, visibly shocked that they had walked straight into a trap.

Flying Squad chief Detective Superintendent Jon Shatford, who led the operation, said, 'They were absolutely startled. They were facing armed officers with guns pointed at them. I don't think they were too happy about that.'

Outside, other officers grabbed the drivers of the getaway boat and lookout van.

Last night Scotland Yard said 12 people in all had been arrested, including alleged accomplices held at addresses in Kent and London.

The astonishing raid attempt could easily have been inspired by the latest James Bond blockbuster *The World is not Enough*, in which the Dome is the backdrop for a dramatic chase sequence involving speedboats.

'Audacious response'

One of the film's stars, Sophie Marceau, was also pictured last year clutching the Millennium Star Diamond, the jewel which played a focal part in the Millennium Eve celebrations when laser beams were fired through its many facets.

Makers Metro Goldwyn Mayer were quick to use the raid to publicise the film. But Mr Shatford refused to be carried away by the hype, saying: 'There has been lots of talk about James Bond but I don't want to glamorise anything the gang has done.

'It was an audacious robbery which could have terrorised members of the public. Fortunately it was foiled by a more audacious police response.'

The drama began at daybreak when police involved in the operation – codename: Magician – began to take up their positions, just as they had done a number of times in the past few weeks.

Those had been false alarms, this time it was for real.

More than 60 members of the public, including schoolchildren rehearsing for a show, were already in the Dome when the arrival of the getaway boat and the lookout van signalled that the raid was about to take place.

The visitors were led to safety by staff who had also been briefed by police. Some were taken to the on site McDonald's restaurant, others to see a Blackadder video.

Within minutes, at 9.30 a.m., the four men aboard the stolen JCB had crashed through the perimeter and Operation Magician was in full swing. The Dome was sealed off and a 100-metre exclusion zone was being set up even as the digger plunged through the plexiglass door, drove past the Learning and Work zones and rammed the entrance to the Millennium Jewels exhibit.

One eyewitness said: 'I heard this enormous crashing noise. My first thought was that something had fallen on top of the Dome – it was so loud. But then I saw this JCB moving towards the Money Zone. I could see two men on it, one driving and the other clinging to the side.'

Café manager Ozcan Ocak said: 'When the JCB came through the wall there was a massive crashing sound. The next thing I knew there was smoke everywhere and the police were running towards it from all directions.

'I saw one police officer, disguised as a cleaner, pulling a gun from a bin bag. It looked like a machine-gun. The police were very heavily armed.'

He added: 'It was very frightening for my customers because some police officers came running towards me screaming, "Get down, get down". Some customers, including an elderly lady, were forced to crouch behind our counter while others hid under tables and behind the staircase next to our café.

'Nobody really knew what was going on, in fact I'm convinced some people thought it was a Millennium Dome stunt.

'When I saw the guns I knew it was very real indeed. I've never felt so frightened in my life.'

Among the visitors were 64 pupils aged 11 to 16 from 23 schools in Dorset. They were there to perform in a show called *Our Town*.

Project assistant Mandy Sylvester said: 'It was very scary. We were just setting up the exhibition profiling Dorset and the show outside the McDonald's Theatre when we were shouted at to "get into the theatre now!"

'I saw a policeman next to me with a gun. The next thing, I heard gunfire and helicopters and everyone in the theatre was terrified.'

While the police faced criticism for allowing children to be exposed to possible danger, they received full backing from both the Dome management and Dorset education officials.

Dome executive chairman David James, said: 'Our concern was the safety of our visitors and the people who work at The Dome. Steps were taken throughout to ensure that our visitors were not put at risk.'

UNDERSTANDING THE TEXT

1 For how long had police known about the plot?

2 How many people were arrested?

3 How many members of the public were in the Dome when the raid began?

4 Using the whole article, write a topic sentence which explains to a new reader what happened at the Dome on 7 November 2000.

INTERPRETING THE TEXT

5 Quite a lot of readers may not understand the headline if they do not know about Ealing comedies.

   a Why do you think the editor of this page wants to compare the robbery to comedy films?

   b What does this tell you about the audience the newspaper is aimed at?

> ## Hints
>
> - Ealing comedies were made in the 1940s and 1950s.
> - They are well known to people of all ages who are interested in the history of films.

6 Look at the way the robbers are presented in the article. Are they shown as:

daring   foolish   dangerous   unlucky?

Choose one or two words that best sum up the way the article presents them. Find some examples from the article to support your choices.

7 Newspaper reports often blend fact with opinion. Look at this sentence from the article:

But a gritty drama of criminal daring swiftly turned into something more akin to an Ealing comedy.

How far is this sentence fact and how far is it opinion? Can you tell the writer's attitude from it? If you were to write the information in a purely factual sentence, how would you express it?

8 The writers describe it as 'the astonishing raid attempt'. Why do you think they include the word 'astonishing'?

9 Some readers may feel that the article contains quite a lot of the authors' own opinions, and also that it makes the raid seem glamorous. Do you agree?

Hints

- Find some examples of where the writers first use words to suggest their own opinions.
- Then say whether you think they make the raid seem glamorous.

LANGUAGE AND STRUCTURE

1 We normally expect the first paragraph of a newspaper article to use a topic sentence – a sentence that tells us the whole story (answering the questions *who, what, where, when?*).

  a How is this paragraph different from what we might expect?

  b How do the writers try to grab our attention with this opening? Do you think it works?

2 The structure of the article is:

  ◆ first describe the raid

  ◆ then give quotations from eyewitnesses.

  a Why do the writers include quotations from eyewitnesses? How would the story be different without them?

b Look at these statements by witnesses:

   i *I heard this enormous crashing noise* (eyewitness)

   ii *It was very scary* (Mandy Sylvester)

   iii *Our concern was the safety of our visitors and the people who work at The Dome* (David James)

Which of these statements:

- feels most informal? How can you tell?
- feels most formal? How can you tell?

3 David James says:

Steps were taken throughout to ensure that our visitors were not put at risk.

This uses the passive voice ('Steps were taken').

  a How could the same idea have been expressed using the active voice, starting like this: 'We …'

  b What difference does using the passive voice make?

WRITING ACTIVITY

Think about why newspaper recounts use quotations from different people involved in a story. Imagine you are covering the story of an attempted burglary at your school. A gang tried to steal 25 computers, but they were foiled by the school caretaker.

Apart from recounting what happened, who would you want quotations from? Remember that newspapers like to use several different points of view where possible.

When you have decided who your quotations would come from, make up the words these people would say. The quotations need to be brief and to the point. Try to make them sound like real spoken statements.

Newspaper investigation
The Lancashire Cat Mystery

Learning objectives

This extract treats an unusual event in an original way. You will be studying these objectives:

- Word level: explore the use of connectives

- Sentence level: vary the formality of your writing; integrate speech, reference and quotation into your writing; develop your paragraphing skills

- Reading: evaluate print, ICT and media texts; explore how media texts influence their readers; analyse the author's standpoint; explore the use of rhetorical devices in texts

- Writing: use language creatively; explore how information texts can be entertaining; use descriptive detail

Introduction

This article reports an event that would probably not be put on the front pages of most national newspapers. Yet it is causing deep concern in a Lancashire village. As you read it, look in particular at the sources of the story – the main people who are quoted and what they say. Decide how reliable you think the whole story is. When you have finished studying this article, you can write one of your own.

In a little Lancashire village, a cat a day is vanishing into thin air. What is going on?

By Ian Herbert, Northern Correspondent

The rumour spread like wildfire through the east Lancashire village of Lumb yesterday. Fourteen cats, so the whisper went, had been seen dead in an isolated country lane. The details were precise, police officers searched, but by nightfall their efforts had come to nothing.

This means the village is still no nearer an explanation to a baffling riddle that is fuelling rumour and counter-rumour. Fifteen cats have vanished here in the space of two weeks from an area of just a few hundred square yards, but no one knows why.

There is an abundance of theories and, in the words of PC Bill King, the neighbourhood officer, 'none of them are pleasant'. The creatures have been taken for the fur trade, say some. A cat killer is on the loose, claim others. There is even a suggestion that the cats have been sold to research laboratories.

Whatever the answer, the saga has left locals living on frayed nerves and the village postmaster's door plastered with photographs of lamented pets. 'We've lost our Chloe, a timid, ginger she-cat,' reads one, between posters for Lumb Baptist Church's football night and a holy beetle drive. 'Missing cat, if seen please telephone,' says another. 'Fluffy, green eyes, very nervous, £200 for safe return.'

The first to vanish from the village, in the Rossendale Valley between Rawtenstall and Burnley, were three rare pedigree Bengals. Two of them, blue-eyed Emma and Ella, were the first snow leopard variety ever bred in Britain and worth £1,250. When they went missing on 2 November, many people believed they had been stolen because of their value.

Their owner, Lisa Shasby, also lost a six-year-old ginger called Axl a week later, though, and it then seemed the cats were being picked off indiscriminately. The Parkinson family on a neighbouring street lost their two-week-old ginger,

Jasper, a week ago. 'Three went on the worst single night,' said PC King.

His own search has taken him through the bed of the nearby Whitewell brook while locals have combed fields in the valley. To have found a dead or injured cat would have been a blessing in some ways, said PC King, who is based at nearby Bacup. 'It is the lack of tangible evidence of these cats which makes us believe something sinister is going on. There's more to this than just "cats will be cats",' he said.

PC King discounts a few more far-fetched explanations. Fifteen years ago, for instance, it was said the Beast of Rossendale roamed these parts. 'There's no danger of that,' said PC King. 'The *Daily Star* also interviewed someone who claimed the "Beast of Bacup ate my Butties" a few years ago but all that's nonsense.'

The charity Pet Search UK said it has never known so many cats go in such a small area though these incidents do follow a case in the Huddersfield suburb of Marsh last month, in which 25 cats fell victim to a poisoner.

In Lumb, 27-year-old Mrs Shasby has just one cat left, a Bengal called Taz. 'I am not letting him out of my sight. He is barricaded inside,' she said.

Last night, as a Lancashire Police spokeswoman confirmed the cats were 'still not accounted for', PC King sent a message to anyone who might try to take a 16th. 'If this person thinks he can come to Lancashire and steal cats he should think again,' he said. 'If he comes back here I'll have him.'

UNDERSTANDING THE TEXT

1 What is the name of the village where the incidents are taking place?

2 How many cats have disappeared so far?

3 What three different theories are there about where the cats are disappearing to?

4 What was the first case of cats disappearing?

5 How many cats disappeared on the worst night?

INTERPRETING THE TEXT

6 Not all newspaper articles are meant to be taken entirely seriously. As you read this article, did you feel that it was a serious news story? Explain your answer.

7 We expect newspaper headings to be short and punchy. This one is not. Unusually, it uses two sentences.

   a What is the headline writer aiming to achieve?

   b How well do you think it works?

   c Think of a headline in a more conventional style.

8 If this were a front page news article, we would expect it to begin with a topic sentence summarizing the whole story.

   a Why do you think it does not do that?

   b Write a topic sentence which would work as a summary.

9 What can you tell about the writer's attitude to the events? Can you tell anything also about his attitude to his readers? (For example, does he know the kind of story they like? Does he aim chiefly to entertain rather than inform them?)

Choose a statement from those below which best sums up what we can say about the writer's attitude. Then write a sentence explaining your choice.

   a It is impossible to tell what the writer's attitude is.

   b The writer is genuinely concerned.

   c The writer treats it as something of a joke.

10 How does the writer make readers want to keep reading? You might mention:

   ◆ the headline

   ◆ the opening paragraph

   ◆ the way he builds tension

   ◆ the quotations he includes.

LANGUAGE AND STRUCTURE

1 Look again at the opening sentence where the author uses a rhetorical device to hook our interest: he might have begun with the phrase '*A rumour*', but instead he writes '*The rumour*'. What is the effect of using the definite article '*the*'?

2 Look at PC King's language. It is quite formal and complex.

It is the lack of tangible evidence of these cats which makes us believe something sinister is going on.

a Why do you think PC King speaks in this formal way? Think about how his language contrasts with that of the other residents.

b If he were just chatting to someone more informally, how do you think the policeman might have expressed the same ideas in a more informal way?

3 Recounts tell us about events in a chronological sequence. They link sentences and paragraphs together with connectives to show one event developing out of another. Write down two or three connectives you notice the writer using.

WRITING ACTIVITY

Look back to the writing activity on page 15. It explored the quotations you might include in a story about a bungled burglary at your school.

Now write the opening of the burglary story, in the way that this newspaper journalist writes about the Lancashire cat mystery. Think of ways to portray the burglars as foolish. Give your school caretaker a very formal style of speech, like PC King. Aim to entertain your readers with a lively recount. You might start with a joke like this:

They thought they'd leave with PCs. Instead the PCs left with them.

or with a dramatic statement like this:

An unusually quiet night for school caretaker Fred Smith was suddenly shattered when …

Extended writing

Create your own recount about a crime for a national newspaper. Use quotations from different eyewitnesses to make it entertaining as well as informative.

You could choose to base your story on the game of Cluedo. Imagine that a murder attempt has taken place in a large old house. A detective arrives and finds a host of unlikely characters:

◆ Reverend Green

◆ Miss Scarlet

◆ Professor Plum

◆ Mrs White

◆ Colonel Mustard

The murder attempt took place in the kitchen with a revolver. The assassin missed her or his target but did not manage to escape from the house. The detective interviewed all the suspects before realizing it was just a game.

The newspaper editor wants you to make this into an entertaining story, with wacky characters and an inefficient police officer.

◆ Think of how you will start your article – the aim will be to make it entertaining, so that readers realize it is a jokey piece.

◆ Think of quotations from the different people involved, including your detective.

◆ Think of how you will structure your article so that you can retell the events of the night.

You could begin like this …

Perhaps the police need to spend a little more time playing board games.

A gunshot was overheard by neighbours at Bagshott Manor in the early hours of yesterday morning. They immediately dialled 999 …

Set out your story as a newspaper article, showing how you would lay out the text, and where you would use a larger text size, bullet points or illustrations.

Travel writing: the essentials

Introduction

Travel writing shows us people and places through the eyes of the writer. Often the setting is exotic – for example, Bill Bryson described going surfing in Australia. Writers might also describe places nearer to home – for example, another famous traveller, Eric Newby, described the exciting memories he had of travelling through Harrods, the London department store.

Travel writing:

- reports on the experiences of going to places and meeting people
- may aim to inform as well as entertain us
- is usually retold in **chronological order**
- usually uses the **first person**
- aims to paint pictures in words, so it may use plenty of **descriptive language**.

Dramatic travel recount
Sinking Fast

Learning objectives

This extract is a very dramatic and entertaining recount of an incident that took place on a journey. You will be studying the following objectives:

- Word level: use terms for analysing language; recognize layers of meaning

- Sentence level: review and develop complex sentences in your own writing; use the full range of punctuation to clarify meaning

- Reading: explore the use of rhetorical devices

- Writing: explore how information texts can be entertaining; integrate varied information into a single account; use descriptive detail

Introduction

This text shows how recounts can be dramatic and full of impact. Steve Callahan is an American yachtsman. In this extract from his book *Adrift*, he is sailing single-handed between England and Antigua in his yacht, *Napoleon Solo*. When you have studied this dramatic recount, you can try writing one of your own.

Glossary

tumultuous – *stormy*

pile driver – *a machine for driving beams of wood, metal or concrete into the ground*

buccaneer – *pirate*

aft pulpit – *a raised, railed-in area at the back of a yacht, from which the sailor has a clear view*

SINKING FAST

It is about 22:30 Greenwich Mean Time. The moon hangs full, white and motionless, undisturbed by the tempest and the tumultuous sea. If conditions continue to worsen, I will have to head more southerly. For the time being, I can do nothing more, so I lie down to rest. At 23:00 I get up and undress. I lie down again clothed only in a T-shirt. A watch circles my wrist, and around my neck is a slab of whale tooth on a string. It is the most I will wear the next two and a half months.

My boat slews around the rushing peaks, her keel clinging to the slopes like a mountain goat, her port side pressed down against the black, rolling ocean. I lie on my bunk, slung upon the lee canvas, hanging as if in a hammock.

BANG! A deafening explosion blankets the subtler sounds of torn wood fibre and rush of sea. I jump up. Water thunders over me as if I've suddenly been thrown into the path of a rampaging river. Forward, aft – where does it come from? Is half of the side gone? No time. I fumble with the knife I have sheathed by the chart table. Already the water is waist deep. The nose of the boat is dipping down. *Solo* comes to a halt as she begins a sickening dive. She's going down, down! My mind barks orders. Free the emergency package. My soul screams. You've lost her! I hold my breath, submerge, slash at the tie-downs that secure my emergency duffel. My heart is a pounding pile driver. The heavy work wrings the air from my lungs and my mind battles with my limbs for the opportunity to breathe. Terminal darkness and chaos surround me. Get out, get out, she's going down! In one rhythmic movement I rocket upward, thrust the hatch forward, and catapult my shaking body on to the deck, leaving my package of hope behind.

Less than thirty seconds have elapsed since impact. The bow points toward its grave at a hesitating low angle and the sea washes about my ankles. I cut the tie-downs that secure the raft canister. Thoughts flash about me like echoes in a cave. Perhaps I have waited too long. Perhaps it is time to die. Going down … die … lost without trace. I recall the life raft instructions: throw the bulky hundred pounds overboard before inflation. Who can manoeuvre such weight in the middle of a bucking circus ride? No time, quickly – she's going down! I yank. The first pull, then the second – nothing, nothing! This is it, the end of my life. Soon, it will come soon. I scream at the stubborn canister. The third pull comes up hard, and she blows with a bursting static *shush*. A wave sweeps over the entire deck, and I simply float the raft off. It thrashes about on the end of its painter. *Solo* has been transformed from a proper little ship to a submerged wreck in about one minute. I dive into the raft with the knife clenched in my teeth, buccaneer style, noticing that the movie camera mounted on the aft pulpit has been turned on. Its red eye winks at me. Who is directing this film? He isn't much on lighting but his flair for the dramatic is impressive.

Unmoving and unconcerned, the moon looks down upon us. Its lunar face is eclipsed by wisps of clouds that waft across it, dimming the shadow of *Solo's* death. My instincts and training have carried me through the motions of survival, but now, as I have a moment to reflect, the full impact of the crash throbs in my head. Never have all of my senses seemed so sharp. My emotions are an incomprehensible mix. There is a wailing anguish that mourns the loss of my boat. There is a deep disappointment in myself for my failures. Overshadowing it all is the stark realization that what I think and feel will not matter much longer. My body shakes with cold. I am too far from civilization to have any hope of rescue.

UNDERSTANDING THE TEXT

1 How would you describe the weather conditions Steve Callahan is facing?

2 Explain what you think the writer means by 'my heart is a pounding pile driver'.

3 Write down two of the emotions Steve Callahan feels towards the end of the extract.

INTERPRETING THE TEXT

4 How does the writer make the yacht seem as if it's alive? Look in particular at the language he uses in the second paragraph.

5 Look at paragraph 3 in more detail.

a How does Steve Callahan use words to recreate the drama of this experience at sea? Look at:

  ♦ his use of vocabulary
  ♦ ways in which he helps the reader to visualize the scene.

b Look at the way he uses sentences to create impact. What do you notice about:

  ♦ his use of very short and much longer sentences? Why does he do this?
  ♦ his mix of statements and questions? What effect does this have?

Write a short paragraph about this.

6 a Look at this sentence:

Unmoving and unconcerned, the moon looks down upon us.

How is the writer presenting the moon here?

> ## Hint
> Look at the use of the verb 'looks down'.

b The writer also uses other rhetorical devices, such as metaphors. Find an example of a metaphor that you think is particularly effective.

7 What picture do you get of Steve Callahan from the extract? Does he seem:

calm   disappointed   angry   aggressive   shocked   uncontrolled?

Choose the word that you think best fits him, and then write a sentence or two explaining why you have chosen it.

LANGUAGE AND STRUCTURE

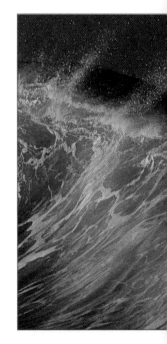

1 Writers use various devices to make their accounts dramatic. Look at this writer's use of punctuation in paragraph 3. Notice how he uses:

♦ capital letters

♦ exclamation marks

♦ dashes.

How do all of these increase the sense of drama?

2 The writer uses some very short sentences: 'My soul screams.' 'I yank.' These are used alongside some much longer sentences. What effect would it create if he used:

a abrupt, short sentences all the time

b longer, more complex sentences all the time?

3 The writer uses vivid language to show us the thoughts going through his mind. Look at the way he uses active verbs to increase the drama:

♦ *my mind **barks** orders*

♦ *the heavy work **wrings** the air from my lungs*

♦ *my mind **battles** with my limbs*

♦ *I **rocket** upward*

a For each of these, think of a different verb the writer might have used (e.g. 'move' instead of 'rocket').

b Describe the different effect of the new word (e.g. 'move' does not have the same sense of speed or rapid movement as 'rocket').

4 Steve Callahan writes a dramatic and often emotional account of being caught in a storm. What would a more factual, less emotional version sound like? Take the main events in the text and write them down in a three-paragraph report, using this frame:

1 Say what we know about the yachtsman.

2 Describe the weather.

3 Describe what happens.

WRITING ACTIVITY

Write about a dramatic moment in your own life, using some of the techniques Steve Callahan uses, such as:

- active verbs

- abrupt, dramatic, short sentences

- onomatopoeic words (e.g. 'bang', 'shush').

Try to show a) what happened and b) the thoughts that raced through your mind.

Your chosen topics might include:

- a time you were involved in an accident

- a time you were terrified of being at a height

- a theme park ride that filled you with terror.

To give your recount maximum impact, aim to use:

- a mix of short and longer sentences

- vivid visual details

- clear description of your own thoughts at the time

- appropriate punctuation, including occasional dashes, capital letters and exclamation marks.

Descriptive travel recount
A Desert Dies

Learning objectives

This extract gives a highly descriptive recount of the traveller's experiences. These are the objectives you will study:

- Word level: recognize layers of meaning
- Sentence level: vary the formality of your writing
- Reading: improve your note-making skills; explore the use of rhetorical devices
- Writing: use language creatively; integrate varied information into a single account

Introduction

In 1985, teacher Michael Asher joined a tribe of desert nomads as they travelled across the Sahara seeking food and shelter. The vast Sahara desert is dying, becoming a waste land, and its people are being forced out.

Like all the best travel writing, Michael Asher's recount gives us personal opinion mixed with strong, vivid description. This extract describes a desert storm. When you have studied the piece, you will be able to write a vivid recount of one of your own journeys.

Glossary

wadi – *a river bed which is dry except in the rainy season*

ochre – *a yellow brown colour*

hobbles – *fastenings put on an animal's legs to limit its movement*

quagmire – *bog*

morass – *bog*

A Desert Dies . . . .

I was woken by a clap of thunder that shook the air like an explosion. Streaks of lightning forked down to the earth, and a second later rain came surging out of the night sky, spattering across the dust in enormous droplets. Within minutes the wadi was inches deep in water, and before we could move, it

was up to our calves. Still heavy with sleep, we tried desperately to shift our gear, but the water rose second by second. 'Hold on to your things!' someone shouted. The water was pouring into the wash from all sides, and for a moment I wondered if we might drown. I stayed where I was, and held on grimly to my saddle-bags, praying that my camera and film would survive. Soon the water was up to my thighs, and I crouched there, trying to keep my balance as the soft sand under my feet began to melt away. I had often heard of Arabs being drowned in wadis by flash floods, and had found it difficult to believe that the water-level could rise so rapidly. I tensed my muscles and stayed without shifting for what seemed like hours as the rain slopped down the back of my shirt. Pieces of twig and tufts of grass nudged against me as they floated downstream in the torrent. I hardly noticed the rain easing off, until it had become no more than a light drizzle. Gradually the water began to subside. By morning it had disappeared completely.

The sickly grey light of dawn crept over the world to reveal a landscape transformed. Everywhere the thorn trees glinted and dripped with moisture, and the grey dust had turned into a rippled carpet of ochre mud that was plastered over the tree trunks. Masses of woody debris and uprooted bushes were piled up along the sides of the wadi. Some of the camels had been half buried in the slime, unable to move because of their hobbles. They sat there, uncomplaining, silently waiting to be released. Many of my things had been carried away. I had lost my sandals, whip, pipe, books and saddle-cushions. My camera and lenses were full of muddy water and most of my film was wet. My maps looked like papier mâché and my tobacco was a pulpy mess. I watched my companions dragging

their gear out of the mud, looking miserable and bedraggled. It was an irony that when rain fell in this thirsty land, it almost always brought greater hardship. None of us was in any mood to celebrate. Wad az Zayadi announced that the flour was soaked and the seasoning ruined. All our leather equipment was waterlogged and our saddles splattered with mud.

'Come on, let's pull the camels out!' Tom said, and we went to inspect the animals. Some of them were stuck tight, where the wadi floor had melted under their weight. We had to go down on our hands and knees in the slime to unfasten their hobbles, then slither about trying to fix their headropes. In places the mud was up to our calves, and we slipped and staggered as we tried to heave the animals out of the quagmire. I hauled on Wad al 'Atiga's rope as Hamid pushed him from the rear. The beast roared and whined in confusion, and suddenly jerked back on the rope so that I plummeted into the mud-slick. Hamid began to laugh uproariously, until he too lost his footing and was sitting up to his waist in the ooze. After that he gave up and started to crawl out of the morass on his hands and knees. It took us more than an hour to drag the slime-sodden animals on to drier ground. They looked a sorry sight, their buff hides covered in slicks of red muck. Afterwards we laid our sheepskins and blankets out to dry, and Wad az Zayadi emptied the flour and seasoning on to plastic sheets. Then we began to hunt for our lost possessions. Most of them were found stuck between the split roots of bushes or covered in mud on the wadi-bed. After another hour I had found all but my pipe. I had begun to despair, when Wad Fadul held it up, grinning. I knocked a pellet of muck out of its bowl and found that it was still smokable.

UNDERSTANDING THE TEXT

1 What surprises the writer about the storm?

2 What is the writer most anxious to save from the flood?

3 How has the storm affected some of the camels?

4 Name two other effects the storm has.

INTERPRETING THE TEXT

5 Look more closely at the first paragraph. How can you tell that the writer really feels afraid of the storm? Pick out the sentence which you think best shows this.

6 What impression do you get of the writer from the text? Write a short paragraph about your response to him. Choose some of the words below if you feel they are appropriate. In your paragraph, aim to support each point with an example.

Word bank

afraid, nervous, apprehensive, cowardly, terrified, bold, courageous, determined, thoughtful, angry, dismayed, worried, bitter, disappointed, confused, concerned for others, compassionate, selfish, patient

7 What picture do you normally have of the landscape of a desert? In what ways does the picture presented in this text differ from that?

8 a What impression do you get of Michael Asher's relationship with the tribespeople? How does he get on with them?

b What impression do you get of his attitude to the camels?

29

LANGUAGE AND STRUCTURE

1 One way writers can make descriptions vivid is by using dramatic language. Look at Michael Asher's description of the storm:

*I was woken by a clap of thunder that **shook** the air like an explosion. Streaks of lightning **forked** down to the earth, and a second later rain came **surging** out of the night sky, **spattering** across the dust in enormous droplets.*

Look at the four highlighted verbs. For each one, look at the different word listed below that the writer might have used:

shook – sounded in
forked – came
surging – falling
spattering – dropping

a Compare the two sets of verbs. Why does Michael Asher's choice of verbs make the storm seem so much more dramatic?

b Michael Asher also uses a simile:

*a clap of thunder that shook the air **like an explosion***

What impression of the thunder does the noun 'explosion' create?

2 Travel writers sometimes use words from the culture they are visiting. Michael Asher uses Arabic words throughout his writing. In this extract he uses the word *wadi*, meaning 'dry river bed'. Some writers might have used the English phrase instead. Why do you think he chooses to use the Arabic term?

3 Look at the start of paragraph 2:

The sickly grey light of dawn crept over the world …

Some writers might have written: 'Dawn was grey …' What picture of the dawn does the writer's image create?

4 Look at the way the writer describes the scene:

Everywhere the thorn trees glinted and dripped with moisture, and the grey dust had turned into a rippled carpet of ochre mud that was plastered over the tree trunks.

This sentence is rich in description. How might you write it in a less descriptive way, so that it communicated only facts?

5 Look at the range of sentences the writer uses in this second paragraph.

◆ Some of them are chiefly description.

◆ Some say what happened next.

◆ Some express an opinion.

Find a sentence that fits each of these functions.

WRITING ACTIVITY

Michael Asher's recount is highly descriptive, helping us to visualize the desert scene, the storm, and the effect it has on the people and camels.

How would a purely factual account of his experiences be different? Imagine that you have been asked to list the events that take place in the extract, but not to give much description.

Reread the text and quickly take down some notes about what happens. Then write a formal recount which simply retells the events. You will probably be able to do this in one paragraph.

Now write a few sentences describing the way you approached this task:

◆ what you were looking for as you took your notes

◆ the main parts of the original text that had to be left out

◆ how you knew which parts of the text to keep

◆ how you made your tone factual.

Unit 2 Extended writing

The description given in recounts helps a reader to see, hear and smell the scene that is being described. This is especially important in travel writing, which aims to create a vivid picture.

Think of a journey you have taken. It does not need to be exotic — it might be quite an ordinary journey, like these:

* your journey to school
* a journey around a supermarket
* a journey to a friend's house.

Your challenge is to bring that journey alive for the reader. Use vivid, descriptive writing to recreate the journey in words. You do not need to write a long piece of work; instead, the emphasis is on very concentrated writing.

Think about the following points:

1 Avoid using the first person all the time ('I noticed the rough road' becomes 'the road is rough and badly mended').

2 Combine description, plot and opinion.

* Description: 'The bike had rusted slightly, and whatever paint had first been applied had now faded into a strange orange grime.'

* Plot: 'I turned the corner, expecting to see box after box of breakfast cereal, but instead …'

* Opinion: 'Every visit to the supermarket leaves me feeling worried — have I spent too much? Have I forgotten something? Was that the right bacon?'

3 Create vivid description by using active verbs (*exploded*, *surging*, *spattering*), adjectives and adverbs, sensuous words (describing sights, sounds, textures, tastes, smells) and similes ('… shook the air like an explosion').

As a starting point, you might begin your account by describing how you closed the door behind you, like this …

I slammed the door behind me. My journey had begun …

How information texts work

Introduction

This unit focuses on the way information texts can combine elements of instruction and persuasion. They will be giving you information, but this is then used as a source of advice.

Information texts describe how things are. They are written for an audience who will usually want to know more about the topic, but may already have some knowledge of the subject.

Information texts should be well ordered and easy to follow, often using **layout features** such as tables and diagrams to help make the information clear. They usually place information in **order of importance**, not chronological order.

Usually they use the **third-person** form to create an impersonal tone, and the **present tense**. Often they use very precise terms, and sometimes **technical language**. The level of technical language will depend on how much the writer thinks the reader already knows about the topic.

Information texts avoid using much descriptive language. They will emphasize **facts**.

Informing and persuading
Vegetarian or Meat-eater?

Learning objectives

Here we compare two examples of information texts that intend to persuade their audience to do something: a leaflet and a web page. You will be studying the following objectives:

- Word level: apply your knowledge of word origins; explore the use of connectives

- Sentence level: develop your paragraphing skills; investigate the organization and conventions of websites

- Reading: gather information from a range of sources; evaluate print, ICT and media texts; compare the way ideas, values or emotions are presented; analyse the author's standpoint

- Writing: use and evaluate a range of presentational devices; explain connections between ideas; integrate varied information into a single account

Introduction

Leaflets are an important way of giving information. A simple leaflet may be a sheet of printed paper, folded in half. More sophisticated leaflets use text and graphics to clarify ideas and, in some cases, to persuade the reader to change his or her opinion or to buy a specific product.

Websites are also an important way of presenting information. As with leaflets, they can use a range of design features to help get their information across to the reader – including interactive techniques and animations.

These two texts take differing views of a similar subject. The first is a Waitrose supermarket leaflet about why we should eat meat and fish. The second is from the website of the Vegetarian Society. It provides questions and answers about choosing not to eat meat.

Both texts aim to do more than just inform us. They both also have persuasive purposes. When you have studied the two texts, you will create a poster that aims to inform and persuade.

Text A

Why we need meat, poultry and fish

Meat is a powerhouse of nutrients. It is a rich source of protein, in a complete form that is easily absorbed by our bodies. Red meat, in particular, is also a good source of easily absorbed iron. Lean meats, especially pork, provide the B vitamins, and liver (chicken, calf and lamb) supplies many nutrients from vitamin A to zinc. Vitamin C, found in vegetables, aids absorption of iron from meat, when eaten at the same meal. However, iron found in non-animal sources, such as vegetables and grains, is less efficiently absorbed by the body.

Poultry is high in protein and is a useful source of B vitamins. It is also low in saturated fat, especially if you remove the skin. In fact, Waitrose skinless chicken breast fillets contain less than two per cent fat.

Fish and seafood are high in protein and packed with nutrients. White fish, such as cod, halibut and plaice, contains less than five per cent fat, while oil-rich fish, such as salmon, mackerel and sardines, is a valuable source of vitamin D.

Who benefits most

Eating meat, poultry and fish can be particularly beneficial at certain times in our lives, when our need for particular nutrients increases. For example, it is important that iron levels are maintained in toddlers and babies who are being weaned, so as to avoid the risk of iron-deficiency anaemia. Teenage girls may also have an increased need for iron at the onset of puberty, as may women who are menstruating. Pregnant women and those who are breast feeding may have an increased need for both protein and iron. As we grow older, our bodies become less efficient at absorbing nutrients, especially iron and vitamin B_{12}. Meat, poultry and fish are good, easily absorbed sources of these.

Meat, poultry and fish provide:

Vital nutrients	Source	Health benefits
Protein	Meat, poultry and fish	Growth and repair
Iron	Meat	Healthy blood cells, and for transporting oxygen around the body
Zinc	Meat, poultry and fish	Healthy immune system and growth
Vitamin B_{12}	Meat, poultry and fish	Healthy blood and nervous system. Vitamin B_{12} is not naturally found in cereals, fruits or vegetables
Vitamin D	Meat and oil-rich fish	Calcium absorption, and strong bones and teeth
Selenium	Meat	Healthy blood cells. It also works in tandem with vitamin E as an antioxidant, to protect cells from the damaging effects of free radicals

What about the fat?

Fat imparts flavour and provides succulence to meat and poultry during the cooking process, so it is fine to leave it on the meat during cooking. To limit your dietary intake of saturated fats, however, it is best to trim off any visible fat, and remove the skin from poultry, particularly before serving. Most of the important nutrients are found in the lean tissue.

Meat can be quite low in fat, with the amount and type depending on the meat and the cut. For example, we sell a variety of mince, ranging from five to 20 per cent fat. Poultry and white fish are both low in fat.

The right balance

To eat healthily, we need to include a wide variety of foods in our diet. Foods rich in protein, such as meat, poultry and fish, are just one element. These should be eaten in balance alongside other important food groups, including fresh fruit and vegetables, dairy foods, and fibre-rich starchy foods such as rice, potatoes, pasta and bread.

To find out more about healthy eating and the different cuts of meat available, visit our website at www.waitrose.com.

Kippers for breakfast

Chicken for lunch

Lamb for dinner

Text B

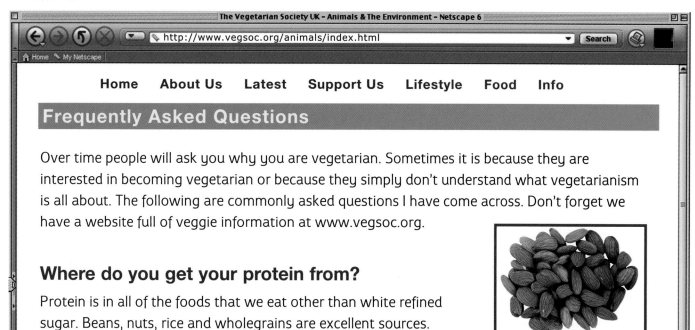

http://www.vegsoc.org/animals/index.html   Search

Home   My Netscape

Home   About Us   Latest   Support Us   Lifestyle   Food   Info

Frequently Asked Questions

Over time people will ask you why you are vegetarian. Sometimes it is because they are interested in becoming vegetarian or because they simply don't understand what vegetarianism is all about. The following are commonly asked questions I have come across. Don't forget we have a website full of veggie information at www.vegsoc.org.

Where do you get your protein from?

Protein is in all of the foods that we eat other than white refined sugar. Beans, nuts, rice and wholegrains are excellent sources.

Say 'nuts' to protein!

If we all went veggie what would happen to the animals?

If we did all go veggie it would happen gradually. The number of farmed animals would also reduce gradually. Therefore it would not be the case that we would have to look after 'spare' farm animals.

What would happen to the farmers?

Vegetarians need farmers too – who do you think would grow the food? Some livestock farmers would move into arable farming while others may move into food-related industries. As with all industries, if the demand for a product goes up numbers employed in that industry will increase. If the demand goes down fewer people will be employed. If we all went veggie more people would be employed in manufacturing vegetarian products.

Can vegetarians get vitamin B_{12}?

Vegetarians get B_{12} from milk and eggs. Vegans can get B_{12} from fortified products such as soya milk or breakfast cereals.

Is vegetarian food more expensive than meat food?

Most pre-cooked foods can be expensive. However, on the whole veggie options do tend to be cheaper, as are restaurant meals. Cooking from basic ingredients is certainly an economical way to live.

School meals are bad enough but the vegetarian options …

The Vegetarian Society has produced school meal planners packed full of delicious veggie recipes. These are available free.

Is a vegetarian diet unhealthy?

No. Every vitamin and mineral is available in a balanced vegetarian diet. What's more, research has compared a healthy veggie diet to a healthy meat diet and the veggie one was found to be the healthiest. (The Oxford Vegetarian Study, 1994). Many top athletes are vegetarians too.

As a meat-eater now I don't need to think about vitamins and minerals. If I went veggie, wouldn't I worry about eating the right sorts of foods?

Both veggies and non-veggies need to think about what they eat. Whatever diet you have, the important issue is balance.

Doesn't cooking vegetarian food take a long time?

What could be quicker than beans on toast?

Home   About Us   Latest   Support Us   Lifestyle   Food   Info

Document: Done

Business ▲ Tech ▲ Fun ▲ Interact ▲

UNDERSTANDING THE TEXT

Start by looking at the two texts separately.

Text A: Leaflet

1 Write down three facts that are included in the text.

2 Look at the first sentence. What does the word 'powerhouse' mean?

3 Look at the end of the first paragraph. Why is iron in meat preferable to iron in other sources?

4 According to the leaflet, how is meat important at three different stages of our lives?

5 Why is fat useful?

Text B: Website

6 Write down three facts that are included in this text.

7 Which single food contains no protein?

8 How can the Vegetarian Society help with school meals?

INTERPRETING THE TEXT

9 Look at the images in the Waitrose leaflet. There are four in total. Why do you think each one has been chosen and what are they supposed to tell us? Describe what each image shows and say why you think it has been included.

Describe the image	Explain why you think it has been chosen

10 Text B uses a question and answer format. Why do you think it uses this format, rather than straightforward paragraphs of explanation?

11 Look again at Text A. Does it seem to be purely an information text, or is it also advertising Waitrose? How can you tell?

> # Hints
> - Look for any references to Waitrose in the text.

12 Who do you think each text is aimed at?

   a vegetarians

   b people thinking of becoming vegetarians

   c definite meat-eaters

   d borderline meat-eaters

   e people generally interested in healthy eating

   f older people

   g younger people

Choose the two categories from the list above that you think are most suitable for each text, and write a sentence explaining why. Structure your answer like this:

Text A	Text B
The two definitions that best describe the target audience are ▲ ▲	The two definitions that best describe the target audience are ▲ ▲
… because …	… because …

LANGUAGE AND STRUCTURE

1 These two texts use some words that are technical (words such as 'nutrients') and some words that are emotive (words such as 'rich' and 'valuable').

   a For each text, find some examples of technical and emotive words.

       Text A   **Text B**

       Technical: Technical:

       Emotive: Emotive:

   b Which text seems to have more of each type of word?

   c Why do you think this is?

2 Look at the way each text addresses the audience. Decide which of the following statements are most accurate:

a Text A uses statements and commands but doesn't really address the audience.

b Text A addresses the reader directly by saying 'you'.

c Text A involves the reader by saying 'you' and talking about 'we', so that it feels straightforward and not patronizing (not talking down to the reader).

d Text A talks down to the reader by using 'you' and 'we' as if the author knows best.

e Text B uses 'you' a lot to address the reader. This makes it feel like a reliable, trustworthy text.

f Text B uses questions to get the reader's interest but doesn't really involve the reader much in any other way.

g Text B uses 'you' and 'we' so that it feels straightforward and not patronizing (not talking down to the reader).

h Text B talks down to the reader by using 'you' and 'we' as if the author knows best.

Now write a sentence or two saying which text addresses the reader in a way that you prefer. Explain why.

3 From looking at the language of the texts, decide:

a which text is more formal

b which is more informative

c which is more complicated

d which involves the reader more

e which is more persuasive.

Explain how you can tell, giving some specific examples.

WRITING ACTIVITY

Using the information from the two texts, put together a poster giving arguments either in favour of becoming a vegetarian or in favour of eating meat. Aim to find eight reasons. Place them in order of most important reason (number 1) to least important reason (number 8). Think about how you will present the information and how you will use language, as well as images, to persuade your readers.

Extended writing

Imagine that Waitrose want to use some of the information from Text B in a future leaflet about vegetarian eating. The leaflet will be aimed at a young audience aged 11 to 14. Waitrose do not wish to use language that is too emotive, because it might upset some people, and also they do not want to put off customers who are happy eating meat.

Take some of the information from Text B, and write it as it might appear in the Waitrose leaflet for young people. Use this title, and then write a one-sided leaflet:

Why you might want to cut down on eating meat

Think about:

◆ how you will present your leaflet – what images and design features you might use

◆ which arguments you might use to persuade readers to cut down the meat content in their diet

◆ how you will use language that is appropriate to an audience aged 11 to 14 – making it clear and informative, without seeming to talk down to them

◆ how you will reword some of the information from Text B.

Speaking and listening
Special assignment

Learning objectives

This special assignment gives you the opportunity to hold a debate on a controversial topic. These are the objectives you will be studying:

- Speaking: compare points of view; use Standard English

- Listening: reflect on your listening skills; analyse bias; identify underlying themes

- Group discussion: review your contributions to recent discussions; evaluate evidence to reach a considered viewpoint; contribute to organizing a group activity

A Initial brief

A group of students at your school has made this proposal to the headteacher:

Based on reliable research, we know that eating too much meat is bad for people. We also know that it involves cruelty to animals and it damages the environment. We therefore recommend that the school canteen should serve meat on only two out of every five days.

You are asked to make a group presentation either supporting this proposal or arguing against it. Your presentation should last five minutes, and will be followed by questions.

Work in a group of three to five. Your teacher will ask you to take up a position – either in favour of or against the proposal. You will have one lesson in which to prepare your presentation.

B Research

1 In your group, brainstorm the arguments you will use to make your case. Use the two texts from Waitrose and the Vegetarian Society which you read on pages 35 to 38. You might also want to do additional research.

2 Make a list of the arguments your opponents will use. Think about how you could counter them.

3 Begin to structure your arguments into a presentation. Who will say what? What different roles will each of you take? Who will introduce your group, and the topic? Who will develop it? Who will conclude?

4 Think about questions you may be asked. Who will respond to them, and how?

5 Plan the format of the presentation in your group. How will you make the topic lively and entertaining, but not trivialize it? Will you use any visual aids? How will you make sure you can speak while making eye contact with the audience, and don't rely too much on notes?

C Practice

Have a practice run-through of your presentation in your group. Give each other feedback on:

- how clearly you spoke

- whether the pace was right

- the way you engaged with the audience (eye contact, body language)

- whether your information and argument were clearly expressed.

D Presentation

Make your presentations. Ask questions after each one.

Afterwards, take a vote on which team gave the best presentation – don't be influenced here by your own beliefs on vegetarianism.

Evaluate the debate.

- How could the presentations have been improved?

- Which persuasive techniques worked best?

- How could arguments have been better presented?

- How could the event have been better organized?

- What have you learned about your own communication skills?

How explanation texts work

Introduction

Explanation texts aim to explain how things work, why things happen, and to give us answers to questions.

They are usually clear and direct, and often begin with a general **opening statement**, then give a **step-by-step** account of an event or process. They often end with a **summary**.

Explanations usually use the **third person** and the **present tense**, but for writing about past events (historical writing) they will use the **past tense**.

Connectives are used to show how one idea relates to another and to indicate cause and effect.

Very precise terms, and sometimes **technical language**, are used in explanation texts, depending on how much the reader is likely to know about the topic.

Explanation texts emphasize **facts and causes**, and do not use much descriptive language.

Explaining a scientific report
Tollund Man

Introduction

This extract is a school worksheet used for history students. It focuses on Tollund Man – the body of a man discovered in a Danish bog on 8 May 1950. Lying on his side, shrivelled, eyes closed, the man from the Tollund Fen was uncovered 2,000 years after his death.

The worksheet is designed to help history students understand more about the investigation into Tollund Man. When you have studied it, you have the chance to write about it in contrasting ways.

The Mystery of Tollund Man

An early Spring day – 8th May 1950. Evening was gathering over Tollund Fen in Biaeldskor Dale in Denmark. The evening stillness was broken now and again by the call of the snipe. Two men were cutting peat for the tile stove and the kitchen range. As they worked they suddenly saw in the peat layer a face so fresh that they could only suppose that they had stumbled on a recent murder. They notified the police at Silkeborg, who came at once to the site. Bit by bit they began to remove the peat from the man's body till more of him became visible. The man lay on his right side just as if he was asleep. He lay 50 metres out from firm ground and had been covered by about 2 metres of peat, now dug away. On his head he wore a pointed skin cap fastened securely under the chin by a hide thong. Round his waist there was a smooth hide belt. Otherwise he was naked. His hair was cropped so short as to be almost entirely hidden by his cap. He was clean-shaven but there was very short stubble on the chin and upper lip.

The air of gentle peace about the man was shattered when a small lump of peat was removed from beside his head. Underneath was a rope, made of two leather thongs twisted together. This was a noose. It was drawn tight around his neck and throat and then coiled like a snake over his shoulder and down across his back.

Who was this man? How long had he lain there beneath the earth? What was the cause of his death?

Scientific report on the body

The body was removed from the bog and examined by doctors and scientists. They came to the following conclusions:

1 Date of burial

Underneath the body was a thin layer of moss. Scientists know that this was formed in Danish peat bogs in the early Iron Age, about the time when Christ was born. The body must, therefore, have been put in a hole in the peat roughly *2,000* years ago in the Early Iron Age. The acid in the peat had prevented the body decaying – it looked as if it had been recently buried.

2 Cause of death

Examinations and X-rays showed that the man's head was undamaged, and his heart, lungs and liver were also well preserved. He was not an old man though he must have been over 20 years old because his wisdom teeth had grown. He had therefore probably been killed by the rope round his neck. This noose had left clear marks on the skin under the chin and at the sides of his neck but there was no mark at the back of the neck where the knot was. It was impossible to tell if his neck had been broken because the bones were very crumbly.

3 His last meal

The stomach and intestines were examined and tests were carried out on their contents. The scientists discovered that the man's last meal had been a kind of soup made from vegetables and seeds, some cultivated and some wild, such as barley, linseed, 'gold of pleasure', knot-weed, bristlegrass and camomile.

There were no traces of meat and from the stage of digestion it was obvious that the man had lived for 12–24 hours after this meal. In other words he had not eaten for a day before his death.

Although such a vegetable soup was not unusual for people of this time, two interesting things were noted:

a) the soup contained many different kinds of wild and cultivated seeds and some of them must have been gathered deliberately, because they were not always easy to find. The soup was, therefore, probably for a special occasion.

b) the soup was made up from seeds which were connected *only with the spring*.

UNDERSTANDING THE TEXT

1 How did scientists work out that the man must have been put in the bog around 2,000 years earlier?

2 How old was he?

3 How could scientists tell his age?

4 What is known about the way he died?

5 What clue was there that a special occasion had taken place?

INTERPRETING THE TEXT

6 What can you deduce from the man's last meal about the community he lived in and their habits?

7 What mysteries are there surrounding the death of Tollund Man?

8 The text contains many factual details.

   a Write down one fact.

   b Does it contain any personal opinions? If so, write them down; if not, explain why not.

LANGUAGE AND STRUCTURE

1 Like most explanatory texts, this one is written in the third-person form. It never uses the pronouns *I* or *me*.

   a Why do you think this is?

   b Would the worksheet be less or more interesting to read if it used a more personal style?

2 Look at the first sentence under the heading 'Scientific report on the body'. It uses the passive voice ('The body was removed … by …').

    a How could the writer have written this sentence using the active voice?

    b Why do you think the passive voice has been used?

3 The worksheet is aimed at students aged about 14. What clues are there in the language that this is the writer's target audience, rather than doctors and scientists?

You might comment on:

 ◆ the length and types of sentences

 ◆ the structure of the explanation

 ◆ the use of vocabulary.

4 Look at the structure of the worksheet:

 ◆ general introduction

 ◆ three sub-headings with explanations beneath each one.

Could the sub-headings ('Date of burial', 'Cause of death', 'His last meal') have been placed in any order, or did it need to be this particular order?

5 Choose two sentences whose meaning is linked, and show how the writer links the ideas in the second sentence back to the ideas in the first. What are the linking words or phrases?

WRITING ACTIVITY

Two different types of writing assignment could be set for students reading this handout. A history teacher could set an essay about the facts; an English teacher could ask for an imaginative account of what Tollund Man might be thinking and feeling.

Write the opening paragraphs of these two assignments.

Assignments:

History	English
Write a factual report about Tollund Man – who he was, what we know about his society, and how he might have been killed.	Imagine you are Tollund Man. You have been dug up after 2,000 years at rest, and scientists are prodding at your body. What thoughts are going through your mind?
Sample starter: Tollund Man was dug from a Danish peat bog dating from …	Sample starter: Light again – it's years since I last saw light …

Write a brief paragraph explaining how you approached the two tasks, and how you chose a style that was appropriate for each.

How successful did you feel each of your openings was in fulfilling its purpose? Were you more skilled at writing in one style than the other?

Unit 4 Extended writing

Use this activity to help you review an essay you have recently written in English or another subject.

A checklist is given below to help you evaluate how well you have written the work. Aim to write four brief paragraphs about the essay, one under each heading.

A Structure

- How have you structured the assignment?
- Why did you structure it in this way?
- Have you given a general statement near the beginning (if appropriate) and then explored different examples?
- Have you used quotations or specific examples to support your ideas?
- Have you shaped your writing into coherent paragraphs?
- Have you used connectives like *another, although, however* to link ideas together?
- How could you have improved the structure?

B Sentences

- What types of sentences have you used – is there a variety of short and long sentences? Have you used only statements, or commands and questions also?
- Have you kept the style factual, rather than descriptive?
- Have you kept the tone impersonal, rather than using 'I' and 'me' too much?
- How could you have improved your use of sentences?

C Words

- How have you used your vocabulary – have you chosen words that are appropriate for the topic?

- Have you used formal vocabulary, and technical words when necessary?

- Have you avoided contractions such as 'isn't' or 'weren't', to create a more formal tone?

- How might you have improved your use of vocabulary?

D Overall evaluation

Write a final sentence or two, saying how effective you feel your assignment is. Be as clear as you can about its strengths and weaknesses.

Parody

Introduction

Once you become familiar with the way different non-fiction texts are written, it can be entertaining to play around with the conventions and rules.

A lot of comedy shows and films do this kind of thing. For example, the *Airplane* movies took the conventions of disaster films and made them funny; comedy programmes like 'Deadringers' imitate news or documentary programmes.

Poking fun at a style of text or programme in this creative way is known as **parody**. This unit looks at one specific example of a parody – the way the magazine *Private Eye* uses the conventions of a newspaper to retell some parts of the story of *Macbeth*.

Parodies often use the conventions of a well-known type of text (e.g. news bulletins, documentaries, newspaper reports) and apply them to unexpected subject matter.

Parody of a newspaper report
The Glamis Herald

Introduction

Private Eye is a satirical magazine. This means that it pokes fun at the government, politicians and celebrities. Sometimes the tone of this is humorous and playful (parody); sometimes it is much more critical (satire). When you have studied this text, you will have a chance to write a parody of your own.

This article uses the conventions of a daily newspaper to present the story of *Macbeth* … which has itself been updated to hint at the former President of the USA, Bill Clinton, and his wife Hillary.

To understand the way the parody works it would be most helpful to know something about Shakespeare's play *Macbeth*. If you have not studied it, you can read a summary of the play on page 59.

Glossary

thane – *knight or duke*

The Glamis Herald

Macbeth defends wife – 'Saintly, selfless public servant' says former Thane

By HENRY THE PORTER

The controversial new king of Scotland, King Macbeth, today spoke out in defence of his wife, Lady Hillary Macbeth, whom many critics have called 'the power behind the throne'.

Cawdor What A Scorcher

At an emotional press conference in the dungeon of the castle, the king told scribes of his deep distress over the recent 'Duncangate' allegations.

- **It is rumoured that the unexpected death of King Duncan, a close member of the Macbeth circle, may well have had something to do with the Macbeths and Lady Macbeth in particular.**

- **It is further claimed that the suicide of long-term Macbeth associate, Banquo, may also have had a political motive.**

But the king firmly rebutted any such reports, saying: 'My wife has the finest moral compass of anyone I know.' He also said that the allegations had left Lady Macbeth very distressed and that she had to call in medical help following attacks of sleepwalking.

Banker's Ghost

There were also unconfirmed reports that the king himself had been subject to hallucinations and that a recent reception at the castle had to be called off suddenly after the king was 'taken ill'. Suggestions that the king may have 'seen ghosts' were dismissed by an official spokesman.

Weather Forecast for Tomorrow and Tomorrow and Tomorrow
With IAN MACBETHKILL

A LARGE area of trees is now on the move in the Birnam area which is expected to reach Dunsinane by tomorrow midday.

Cooking Tips
With THE WEIRD SISTERS

TAKE ONE Eye of Newt, one Toe of Frog, one Wool of Bat and one Tongue of Dog. Bring to the boil and put in the microwave in a non-metallic receptacle.
(Shurely shome mishtake?)

On Other Pages

UNDERSTANDING THE TEXT

1 Write down two features which make the text look like a real newspaper.

2 What is the gist of the 'story' that the text is reporting?

3 Who is Banquo, according to the article?

4 Why is Hillary Macbeth upset?

INTERPRETING THE TEXT

5 The text makes a lot of jokey references to *Macbeth*. Imagine the newspaper is being read by someone who does not know Shakespeare's play. Choose one of the examples below and explain the joke:

  a The recent 'Duncangate' allegations

  b Weather Forecast for Tomorrow and Tomorrow and Tomorrow

  c Cooking Tips with the Weird Sisters

6 The text also makes reference to ex-President Clinton and his wife. What does the author's style suggest about his attitude towards them?

7 These are some of the features we expect in newspapers. For each one, write down an example from this text.

Feature	Example
Headline to grab the reader's attention	
Byline (telling us the name of the writer)	
Sub-headings to break up the text	
A topic sentence which tells the whole story at the start of the article	
Trails for other features in the newspaper	
Advertising	

8 Write a short paragraph about your response to the text.

   a What do you like about it? Which jokes do you find funny? Which bits do not make sense? How could it be funnier?

   b What does it suggest to you about the writer's attitude to powerful politicians, and the way they are usually presented in newspaper reports?

LANGUAGE AND STRUCTURE

1 Newspaper headlines often have certain key features. Look at the features below and write down an example from this text.

   a They use the present tense.

   b They use alliteration (repetition of initial consonants).

   c They are telegrammatic – they miss out grammatical words like *the, his* and *their.*

2 The sentence style in newspapers often uses a lot of modification. This means giving as much detail as possible in each sentence. Take this sentence:

An English teacher today bought a new car.

Reported in a newspaper, this might begin:

Trendy English teacher Jez Foley, 24, yesterday amazed pupils at Long Melford High School …

Notice how the writer uses labels ('trendy', '24') to add details to the subject of the sentence.

Now look at the first sentence of the *Glamis Herald.* How does the writer use a similar technique in writing about Macbeth?

3 Newspapers sometimes use the passive voice, like this:

Suggestions that the king may have 'seen ghosts' were dismissed by an official spokesman.

   a Write this sentence in the active voice.

   b Why do you think newspapers sometimes use the passive voice in this way?

4 Some of the writing in the text is funny because of its reference to *Macbeth* or the Clintons. Some is funny because it uses word play or puns.

Choose one example from those below and explain how the writer is playing with words:

a Cawdor What A Scorcher

b Angus McDeayton

c Ian Macbethkill.

WRITING ACTIVITY

Write your own headline and topic sentence for a spoof newspaper article using one of these examples:

◆ the Shakespeare play you are reading

◆ another text you have recently read

◆ a fairy story or legend.

Look back at your answers to the questions above to remind yourself of the key features of headlines and newspaper style.

Summary of *Macbeth* by William Shakespeare

Macbeth wins honour in battle for Scotland. Afterwards, Macbeth and his fellow officer Banquo meet some witches stirring their cauldron on the battlefield. They prophesy that Macbeth will gain a new title, and that later he will become king of Scotland. When Macbeth and Banquo present themselves to King Duncan, he decides to reward Macbeth with the title Thane of Cawdor, but he declares his own son, Malcolm, to be the heir to the kingdom.

King Duncan then visits Macbeth's castle. Macbeth is driven on by his wife to kill the king that night. When the king is found stabbed, Banquo and another lord, Macduff, begin to suspect Macbeth.

Macbeth becomes king. He then arranges the murder of Banquo, without Lady Macbeth's knowledge. At a ceremonial banquet that night, Banquo's ghost appears to Macbeth and the meal is disrupted. Macbeth meets up with the witches again, who tell him of further prophecies. He feels sure that he can get rid of all possible enemies and remain as king.

Macbeth sends attackers to Macduff's castle, and Lady Macduff and her children are killed. Macduff himself has already escaped and he becomes Malcolm's ally. Lady Macbeth dies, deranged by guilt and grief, and Malcolm's troops advance towards Macbeth's besieged castle. All the witches' prophecies are shown to be tricks, and Macbeth is killed in the battle – his head is brought to Malcolm by Macduff. Order is restored for Scotland, and Malcolm becomes king.

Extended writing

Choose a non-fiction genre and write a parody of a text you know well. For example, you could choose:

♦ a news report on the feud between the Capulets and the Montagues, including on-the-spot interviews with the fathers of Romeo and Juliet

♦ an encyclopedia entry for Hogwarts School, or another famous location from a book you have read

♦ a page from an instruction book on how to care for angels (based on *Skellig*).

Other possible text types:

♦ an extract from a school textbook

♦ a report of an event or experiment

♦ sports journalism or commentary

♦ a speech

♦ a newspaper editorial.

Hints

● To make it entertaining, match your text type with an unusual topic, such as one of those listed above.

● To make it funny, treat the topic seriously (e.g. write your instructions on caring for angels as if they are deadly serious). Include vivid details to bring your topic to life.

● Remind yourself of the language features of the text type you are using – for example, by looking back at the introduction pages for text types in this book.

● Do not aim to write too much – the focus should be on the quality of your parody, not the amount you write.

Assess Your Learning

Unit 1 Media recounts

Evaluate the recount you produced for the extended writing task on page 20. Share your writing with a partner. Discuss it in order to finish the following sentences:

- *To make my recount entertaining I …*
- *A good example of description is …*
- *I brought the characters to life by …*
- *To link ideas together, I used the following connectives …*
- *Overall, I am pleased with …*
- *Next time, I would aim to improve …*

Unit 2 Travel writing

1 Look at the travel writing you produced for the extended writing task on page 32. Copy and complete this grid to help you assess your work.

Features	Example
Avoided using the first person	
Told events in order (plot)	
Gave an opinion	
Created vivid description	

2 a What are you most pleased with about your writing?

b What would you like to do better next time?

Unit 3 Information texts to persuade

1 Think carefully about how your reading skills are developing. Look back at your response to Texts A and B. Copy the grid below and tick the columns you think describe your skills.

Reading skills	Easily	Sometimes	With difficulty
I can find information in the text and record it accurately (Understanding the text questions 1 to 8)			
I can explain my interpretation of the text clearly (Interpreting the text questions 9 to 12)			
I can make detailed comments about the writer's use of language and structure (Language and structure questions 1 to 3)			

2 Choose one of these skills and explain how you could improve your responses.

Unit 4 Explanations

This table focuses on reading skills and the strategies that good readers use. With a partner, discuss your own reading skills. Decide which skill you wish to develop and explain how you will improve that skill.

Skill	Strategies that good readers use	My target
Skim	▲ Read quickly ▲ Identify key points ▲ Use headings, topic sentences and pictures to gain an overview	
Scan	▲ Keep key words in mind ▲ Concentrate on one thing at a time ▲ Know which part of the text to search in	
Interpret meanings	▲ Understand the significance of the writer's deliberate choice of words ▲ Look for meanings beyond the literal sense ▲ Ask questions of the text	
Identify the writer's viewpoint	▲ Identify fact and opinion ▲ Recognize bias ▲ Notice details the writer has chosen to emphasize or leave out	

Unit 5 Playing with non-fiction conventions

Think about your performance of the nursery rhyme news report in the starter activity on page 8. Use traffic lights to review your speaking and listening work.

● I need to develop this.   ◐ I did this quite well.   ○ I did this very successfully.

In preparing, how well did you:	
explain your ideas to the group?	○
support teamwork by organizing, solving problems and considering alternatives?	○
listen to and develop other people's suggestions?	○

In performing, how well did you:	
use Standard English?	○
speak in an appropriate style?	○
respond to what was said by others?	○

Persuade and Analyse

Getting started
Unit 6 Persuasive writing

In newspapers and magazines, there is often a mix of writing types, depending on the subject and approach of each article. Some texts are mainly factual and aim to give a balanced, fair view of a topic. Others are highly opinionated and are written to persuade the reader towards a specific viewpoint or action.

1 Read the article headings listed in the grid below and decide what sort of writing is likely to follow them.

Article headings	Balanced, informative writing	Highly persuasive writing	Could be either
Fishing as a hobby should be banned			
Weather forecasting and how it works			
Why voting at elections is important			
Vandals should face harsher punishment			
Stop panicking about crime			
How wine is made			

2 Think up two more article headings, one of which would be followed by persuasive writing, the other by balanced, informative writing.

Unit 7 Analytical writing

Analysis texts usually contain facts and statistics which need to be presented clearly and accurately. Most readers find it easier to absorb information that is given in a variety of ways (e.g. in text and graphics) than in one form only.

1 Imagine you are presenting the results of a survey about a subject of your choice. For example: 'How students in your class spend their leisure time', 'How students in your class spend their pocket money'.

With a partner, plan the research that you need to do, using a spider diagram. Focus on the aspects that you will research rather than the order of the material at this stage. Your diagram might start something like this:

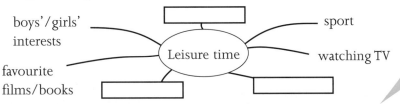

boys'/girls' interests

sport

Leisure time

watching TV

favourite films/books

2 Now list the variety of ways in which you might present your analysis. Remember that text can be presented in different ways, and there is a wide range of graphics which can display facts and statistics.

Unit 8 Advice texts

Advice can be formal or informal, depending on the subject and who it is for.

1 Read the situations below and decide the level of formality that the advice requires in each situation. Shade in the appropriate number of circles: one circle for very informal; five circles for very formal.

2 Compare your levels of formality with a partner or the rest of the group. Be prepared to justify your chosen level of formality for each situation.

Situation	Level of formality
a Telling a friend some bad news about a relative	○○○○○
b Telling a parent that you're in trouble at school	○○○○○
c Telling a teacher that you have forgotten to do your homework	○○○○○
d Telling a friend that you have forgotten to do your homework	○○○○○
e Someone in assembly giving advice on personal safety	○○○○○
f A leaflet in the dentist's on how to look after your teeth	○○○○○
g A dentist advising a terrified patient that if he doesn't clean his teeth better then he will need fillings	○○○○○
h A teacher telling a student how to improve her netball skills	○○○○○

Unit 9 Reviews

Reviews can help people to decide whether to read a book, see a film, or go to a play. They need to catch the reader's attention, then go on to be informative and entertaining.

1 Read these opening sentences of reviews of *Harry Potter and the Half-Blood Prince*. They were all written by Year 9 students.

2 Which review would you most want to read further? Remember, a good review does not necessarily have to be in favour of the product.

Kim
Harry's back, and this time his life is under threat as never before ...

Matt
The title may not roll off the tongue easily, but the pages turn quickly when you get started on this latest book in the series ...

Iqbal
I think I may be getting too old for Young Master Potter ...

Karensa
This is undoubtedly J.K. Rowling's best novel yet ...

Tom
I didn't enjoy this book one bit ...

Terry
Uh-oh - another Harry Potter book has arrived ...

How persuasive texts work

Persuasive language is used in letters, essays, advertisements, leaflets, television programmes, newspaper editorials and opinion pieces. Writers may aim to:

- express a point of view
- change your opinions
- get you to buy something
- persuade you to join an organization.

The text may use **illustrations** and different **layout features** to make an impact. The writing is often structured with an **opening statement**, and then **key points** will be described in more detail. The reader will be guided through the argument by **logical links**, and the writer may use **humour** to appeal to the reader.

Persuasive texts often use the **first person** to express opinions, but may use the **third person** to create a more impersonal effect. Advertising might be directly addressed to the reader by using the **second person** and **imperatives**. Persuasive writing will usually be **active**, use short sentences for effect, and be written in the **present tense**.

Writers will choose **emotive words** in an attempt to influence the reader, and **word play** may be a feature of advertisements.

Getting audience attention
RSPCA Radio Advertisement

Learning objectives

This text is the script for a radio advertisement that aims to capture listeners' attention and sympathy. These are the objectives you will be studying:

- Word level: recognize layers of meaning
- Sentence level: analyse and use conventions of different text types
- Reading: explore how media texts influence their readers
- Writing: use and evaluate a range of presentational devices; present a case persuasively
- Speaking and listening: compare points of view

Introduction

Advertising is usually designed to entertain or inform us as well as to persuade. It is not always trying to sell us a product – sometimes advertising campaigns aim to change our opinions, or to teach us something new.

This text is a transcript of a 60-second radio commercial made by an advertising agency for the RSPCA, a charity that aims to prevent cruelty to animals.

As you read, look at the way language is used to persuade listeners – and remember that the text was written to be heard on the radio, not read on the page. When you have studied it, you can write an advertisement of your own.

Glossary

VO – *voice over*

MVO – *male voice over*

RSPCA Radio Advertisement

60 seconds

SWIM

VO: We are going swimming, my brother and I. We are going swimming with our best friend. But our best friend has not brought a towel. He has brought a sack. We are going to swim in the river even though it is very cold at this time of year. My brother and I run down the tow path. I can see my breath in front of my face. We are happy to be running as we don't get taken out as often as we used to. Our best friend seems to have less time these days. Now we are at the river. Suddenly my brother and I don't feel like swimming any more. It is cold. It is so cold that our best friend puts us in the sack to keep warm. I hope he does not slip because it would be very difficult to swim in this small sack.

MVO: Every year the RSPCA has to rescue thousands of unwanted animals.
    If you give a damn, don't give a pet.

UNDERSTANDING THE TEXT

1 The speaker describes the way things have changed in his or her life. Name two of them.

2 Who are the speaker and brother?

3 Who is the best friend?

4 How can you tell that the weather must be very cold?

5 Explain in a sentence what is happening in the first section of the text.

INTERPRETING THE TEXT

6 At which point did you work out who the speaker was in the first part of the text?

7 What hints are there about what will happen eventually?

8 What hints are there that the speaker is very trusting of the best friend?

LANGUAGE AND STRUCTURE

1 The script is designed to be spoken. How far do you think the language feels like spoken language? Look at sentence structures and vocabulary.

2 How does the writer keep us uncertain at first about who the speaker and 'best friend' are?

3 The commercial tells a story using the present tense ('We are going swimming …'). This is fairly unusual for stories, which are more often told in the past tense ('We were going swimming …'). Why does the writer choose to tell the story using the present tense?

4 a How is the language of the last section ('MVO') different from that of the first speaker?

b What is the function of this last section of the advertisement?

5 Advertisements often use a slogan to summarize their message.

a How effective do you find the slogan: 'If you give a damn, don't give a pet'?

b Who do you think the text is aimed at when it says 'you'? Is the audience general, or is there a specific age group or interest connecting the listeners?

6 This advertisement raises issues about pets and their owners.

In pairs, discuss the arguments for and against:

a owning pets

b giving pets as presents.

Make notes of the different points of view expressed.

WRITING ACTIVITY

How would you present the message of this radio advertisement
in a poster or magazine advertisement?
What image would you use? What would your text say?

Draft a print version of an advertisement for the RSPCA.
Use the same final slogan: 'If you give a damn, don't give
a pet.' Decide on your layout, font style and sizes, and any devices
such as bullet points that you will use to get your point across.

Expressing strong views
Moving Target

Introduction

The writer of this text has strong views about car drivers and expresses them forcefully. Look at the way he constructs his argument and uses language to shape our opinions. When you have studied this opinion piece, you can write one of your own.

Moving Target

by Joe Gardiner

Roads aren't just built for cars. An irate cyclist pulls himself out of the gutter to remind car drivers of their selfish ways.

We wear the same kind of clothes, you and me; drink in the same bars, listen to the same kind of music. You could be my brother, mother, sister, or lover, but I hate you. While you are behind the wheel of your car you are everything I love to loathe – unobservant, inconsiderate, uncaring and above all, in the way. You see, I'm a cyclist.

Tell me, what do I have to do to get your attention? I've forked out £150 on a fluorescent jacket, I've got a halogen headlight, Scotchlight stickers on my crash helmet and enough flashing back lights that you'd mistake my seat-post for a school disco. But, like the plain girl or boy you're probably dating, nobody ever seems to notice me. Here's a tip – when you're opening your car door, look to see if there's anything coming, then look again to see if *I'm* coming. If you're looking for cars, you'll see cars. But you won't see a cyclist. So make like they did in the Seventies: 'Think once, think twice, think bike.'

As if this blinkered vision were not enough, I also have to contend with your selfishness. Not you? Well, see if this rings any bells – you're in a queue of traffic and there's someone waiting to turn right out of a left-hand side street – you're a considerate road-user so you wave them out. Tell me, do you ever look in your wing mirror to see if I'm coming up on the outside? No, I didn't think so. Remember, just because you're stuck in a jam doesn't mean that everyone is.

And aren't those cycle paths fantastic … for parking in? You might think so, but I've heard that doing so can result in your tyres deflating. I've no idea how it happens, but don't be too surprised if you leave your car parked in one and come back to find it with one or more flat tyres than you have spare.

Blind, self-centred … did I mention lacking in foresight? Here's a quick quiz – you're turning right at a T-junction, do you: (a) Stop behind the line, look both ways to ensure the road is clear then pull out; (b) Over-run the line by a couple of feet, stop, glance in each direction then turn; or (c) Roll out to the middle of the road while looking left, force the oncoming traffic to stop and make space for you, then pull away as fast as you can. From what I've seen, most of you think the correct answer is (c) although you'll occasionally be a little more considerate and go for option (b). If I had a quid for every time I had to swerve or stop to avoid being hit broadside by drivers pulling out of a junction I'd have binned my bike in favour of a personal helicopter. Once I've got up speed and gained momentum, I don't particularly relish having to slam on the brakes to avoid coming through your driver's side window. If I was a bus you wouldn't dream of pulling out.

That's not to say I don't enjoy the thrills of having to react with the speed of a cat to your clumsy steering. Mentally alert, I'm poised for reaction, the adrenaline racing through my veins as I tear up the miles. If I underestimate your gross stupidity and end up biting the kerb, I'll wear

my red badge with courage and pride and swap tales of pedal-power derring-do with my fellow cyclists.

A tale that crops up regularly is of you aggressively accelerating then swerving to overtake. This seems to be a favourite manoeuvre when you can see traffic blocking your way just ahead. Traffic should leave me free to sail effortlessly past, except that you seem to delight in positioning yourself on the road in such a way that I end

up stuck as well. Or, you just whip past, slam on the brakes and turn left, leaving me at a standstill in the gutter. That gesture you'll see me making means: 'Mmm … nice driving.'

Which reminds me – when I 'compliment' your road skills in this way then you probably deserve it. There really is no need for you to answer back or jump out of your car and try to batter me. Although the chances of you catching me on your pudgy, car-softened legs are small and the sight of you trying always gives me a laugh.

There you are, I don't like you and you probably don't like me either, but now that you know how much I 'enjoy' seeing you drive like an idiot, you know what to do. Improve your driving and show some consideration to me and other vulnerable road-users: motorcyclists, horse-riders and the like. Go on, you know it'll make me miserable having nothing to moan about.

UNDERSTANDING THE TEXT

1 What is the writer's main complaint about car drivers?

2 Who is he addressing in this article?

3 What steps has he taken to make sure he cycles safely?

4 Find an example where the writer uses sarcasm to make his point.

5 Find an example where the writer uses an angry tone.

INTERPRETING THE TEXT

6 Using a spider diagram, write down some of the complaints the writer makes about car drivers. Then circle the complaints which are most serious (e.g. pulling out of a junction in front of cyclists). Underline the complaints he has which are more minor (e.g. their legs are pudgy and soft).

7 Do you find the article funny, or too aggressive, offensive, insulting, excessive ('over-the-top')? Write about your response to the writer's comments.

8 The writer makes a lot of criticisms, but does he suggest anything constructive? Apart from poking fun at drivers, what do you think his aim is?

9 What impression do you gain of the writer's character?

Hints

- Look at what he says about himself.
- Look at the tone of the language he uses – what does this show about the way he feels?

LANGUAGE AND STRUCTURE

1 The writer uses an unusual style for his argument. He addresses himself to an imaginary reader and uses the second-person form: 'You could be my brother ...'

What if the article was written in the third person, like this: 'Car drivers and I wear the same kind of clothes …'?

a Choose one paragraph and rewrite it using the third person.

b Say how the text feels different in the third person, and why you think the writer probably chose the second-person form.

2 Persuasive texts can use a very direct, informal style to get points across. This text sounds as if the writer is talking to us directly. Find an example of the way he uses language that sounds like spoken English.

3 The writer uses a wide range of punctuation, including quotation marks, ellipses (dots), dashes, and colons. Choose a sentence with one or more of these features and say how the punctuation helps the writer to express his ideas.

4 As with most persuasive texts, the writer builds his argument around a number of connectives and linking words. He uses informal phrases such as:

tell me   *as if*   *that's not to say*   *which reminds me*

a How do these links make his argument seem more personal and informal?

b The final paragraph begins: 'There you are …'
Do you think this is an effective way to introduce the writer's summing up of his arguments?

WRITING ACTIVITY

Imagine you are a responsible car driver who has just read Joe Gardiner's article. You think it is very unfair. You think cyclists also often behave badly on the road. Write a reply to Joe Gardiner, expressing the driver's point of view.

As in his article, use the first person to express your opinions, and the second person to address your reader directly.

Extended writing

Choose a topic that you feel strongly about. Some suggestions for topics are given below.

Your aim is to write an opinion piece like Joe Gardiner's, in which you have your say about a subject on which you have strong opinions.

Possible topics

- Why attending school should be an optional form of education – people can learn just as well at home via TV, home study and the Internet.

- Why you should be given more freedom at school or at home – to behave like an adult you have to be treated like an adult, and given responsibility for taking your own decisions.

- Why people who smoke should be made to pay for their own medical treatment – so that there would be more money to spend on people with other illnesses.

When you have chosen your controversial topic, structure your main ideas into the order you will write about them. Think of the arguments you will use to persuade your readers.

Practise your style: Joe Gardiner addresses his readers directly, 'buttonholing' them with his ideas. Test your style in a few opening sentences, like this:

I'm sick of being treated like a child. I'm not a child. You tell me not to be childish. Then what do you do? Talk to me as if I've got a dummy in my mouth . . .

Surely there can't be many people on earth who don't know about the damage smoking is doing. You can't open a magazine without seeing a health warning. 'Cancer sticks, coffin nails' – isn't this what people who smoke call their cigarettes? Well, if you know how bad cigarettes are, isn't it your choice whether you smoke them?

Remember:

♦ The aim is to write something hard-hitting, lively, but not offensive – offending your audience will not persuade them of your point of view.

♦ You are not aiming to give a balanced view, but to get your own ideas across.

♦ Use the first- and second-person forms.

♦ Use emotive, dramatic vocabulary, and perhaps humour.

♦ Use commands, questions and statements for variety.

♦ Start with an opening statement and then move through key points, one per paragraph.

Speaking and listening:
special assignment

Learning objectives

This special assignment gives you the chance to hold a debate about road use. You will be studying the following objectives:

- Speaking: use Standard English

- Listening: compare points of view; identify underlying themes

- Group discussion: evaluate evidence to reach a considered viewpoint

Debate on traffic

Based on Joe Gardiner's opinion piece, have a group debate on this motion:

It's time to get cars off Britain's roads.

Work in small groups to prepare opposing views for the debate. Different groups could represent different interest groups:

- Car drivers (who enjoy the freedom of car travel)

- Cyclists (who want a safer, more environmentally friendly transport system)

- Walkers (who want less pollution, less noise and less traffic)

- Rail companies (who want more business for trains)

- Coach companies (who fear they may lose business because of heavy traffic, unless cars are limited and coaches encouraged)

- Building contractors (who want to keep building roads)

Each group should put together the main points of their argument ready for the debate. Decide who is speaking about each point. Then hold your debate with each group having the chance to make its case, followed by questions.

Finally, try to come to an agreement about whether cars should be limited and, if so, to what extent.

How analytical texts work

Analytical texts aim to give a considered response to other texts, to products such as consumer goods and media broadcasts, or to events. In schools, analytical texts are often written in the form of essays.

Analysis is often structured like this:

opening statement

↓

discussion of the issue in general terms

↓

exploration of key points in turn

↓

summary or conclusion

♦ The style is usually impersonal, using the **third person**. The **first person** might be used for giving personal opinions in the conclusion.

♦ Texts are usually written in the **present tense**.

♦ **Connectives** help the reader to compare and contrast ideas and to follow the logic of the arguments.

♦ Analytical texts will often use the **specialist vocabulary** of the subject under review (e.g. historical or scientific terms).

♦ Vocabulary describing **judgements** will also be used, with adjectives such as *involving, thought-provoking*.

Giving evidence and opinion
Road Transport

Learning objectives

This text is from the website of a pressure group, analysing some of the problems that are the subject of its campaigns. These are the objectives you will be studying:

- Word level: use different ways of checking words

- Sentence level: integrate speech, reference and quotation into your writing; develop your paragraphing skills

- Reading: gather information from a range of sources; evaluate print, ICT and media texts

- Writing: develop ideas through writing; explain connections between ideas; offer advice in an impersonal style; present a balanced analysis

---

Introduction

The text featured here discusses the problems of road traffic. It comes from the website of Friends of the Earth, a pressure group that campaigns to improve the quality of the environment.

This document analyses the damage road transport is doing to the environment. It uses facts and statistics to support its case. It finishes with suggestions for what readers can do to help. When you have studied it, you can write an analytical text of your own.

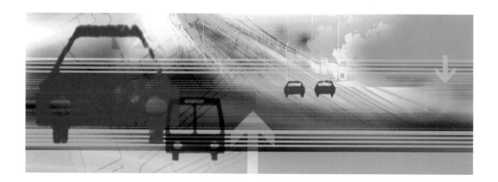

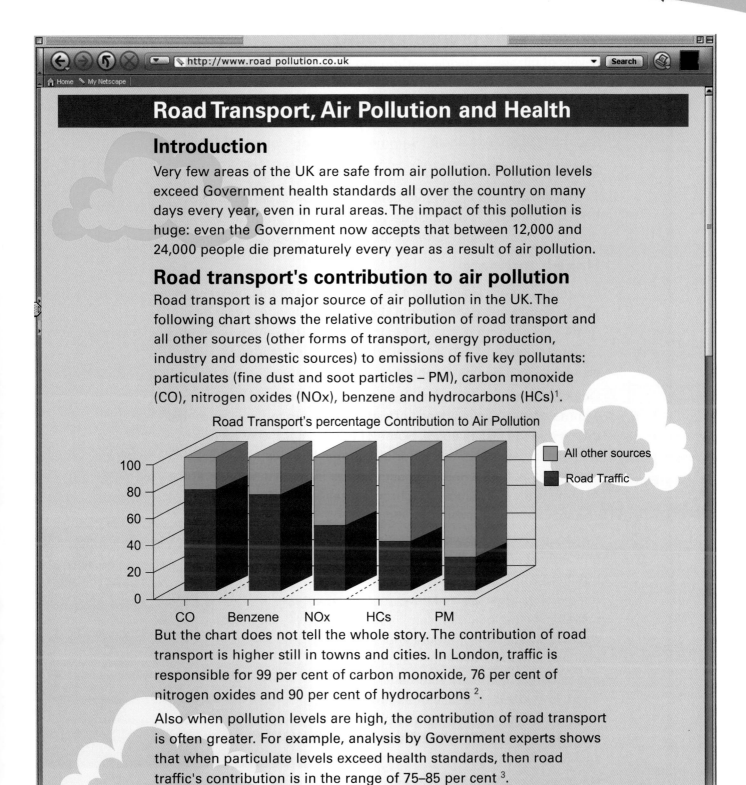

Road Transport, Air Pollution and Health

Introduction

Very few areas of the UK are safe from air pollution. Pollution levels exceed Government health standards all over the country on many days every year, even in rural areas. The impact of this pollution is huge: even the Government now accepts that between 12,000 and 24,000 people die prematurely every year as a result of air pollution.

Road transport's contribution to air pollution

Road transport is a major source of air pollution in the UK. The following chart shows the relative contribution of road transport and all other sources (other forms of transport, energy production, industry and domestic sources) to emissions of five key pollutants: particulates (fine dust and soot particles – PM), carbon monoxide (CO), nitrogen oxides (NOx), benzene and hydrocarbons (HCs)[1].

Road Transport's percentage Contribution to Air Pollution

But the chart does not tell the whole story. The contribution of road transport is higher still in towns and cities. In London, traffic is responsible for 99 per cent of carbon monoxide, 76 per cent of nitrogen oxides and 90 per cent of hydrocarbons [2].

Also when pollution levels are high, the contribution of road transport is often greater. For example, analysis by Government experts shows that when particulate levels exceed health standards, then road traffic's contribution is in the range of 75–85 per cent [3].

Road transport is also the main cause of ozone (summertime smog). Ozone does not come directly from vehicles or factories but is created by chemical reactions between nitrogen oxides and hydrocarbons.

Where is the problem worst?

Levels of nitrogen dioxide, carbon monoxide, hydrocarbons and particulates are highest in towns and cities, where there is more traffic. But this does not mean that rural areas do not have a problem. Levels of summertime smog are worst in rural areas. See the FOE briefing sheet "Summertime Smog" for more details.

Who is at risk?

The health of up to one in five people in the UK is particularly at risk from air pollution. These include young children, pregnant women, the elderly, and people suffering from heart and lung diseases.

Health impacts

In a recent report, Government experts concluded that between 12,000 and 24,000 people might die prematurely every year as a result of short-term exposure to air pollution. The report added that a further 14,000 to 24,000 hospital admissions and readmissions may also be caused by this air pollution [4].

One of the most well-known impacts of air pollution is an increase in asthma attacks. The incidence of asthma appears to have more than doubled in the last 15 years. Some of this increase may be due to changes in how doctors categorise asthma, but it is now widely accepted that the incidence of asthma has increased considerably. Asthma is the most common chronic disease of childhood with around one in seven children affected.

Evidence of a link between pollution and asthma is certainly accumulating, but there is no proof yet of a causal relationship. What we do know, however, is that pollution can aggravate asthma symptoms and can also trigger an asthma attack in people who are already asthmatic. There is evidence that use of asthma medication and hospital admissions diagnosed as asthma increase during severe pollution episodes.

Government health experts have concluded that 'there is a consistent, though modest, association between exposure to traffic and asthma prevalence in children' [5]. Other researchers have found that people living in streets with heavy traffic tended to suffer more illness than residents of streets with light traffic [6]. Similar studies in other countries have shown a relationship between the amount of traffic in an area and people with respiratory symptoms or wheeze [7].

How much does it all cost?

The impact of air pollution on health can also be assessed in monetary terms: the cost of health care, the cost of days of work lost, the economic cost of premature deaths. The National Asthma Campaign has estimated that asthma costs the UK over £1 billion per year [8]. Environmental economists have estimated the cost of air pollution from road transport at £19.7 billion per year [9].

What you can do

You can play your part in cutting air pollution from traffic:

- Cut your car use.
  Use alternatives such as public transport, cycling and walking.

- We are trying to encourage the Government to adopt policies which will deliver traffic reduction by encouraging MPs to sign Early Day Motions – on Company Car Tax, 'home zones' and CO_2 emissions. PLEASE WRITE TO YOUR MP, asking them to sign these motions.

- Join Friends of the Earth and help us campaign for traffic reduction and cleaner cars.

Notes

return to text

1. Department of Transport: Transport Statistics Great Britain 1996

[Benzene figures from: Department of the Environment National Air Quality Strategy (1997)]

return to text

2. The Ashden Trust How Vehicle Pollution Affects Our Health (1994)

return to text

3. Quality of Urban Air Review Group Airborne Particulate Matter in the United Kingdom (1996) page 146

return to text

4. Committee on the Medical Effects of Air Pollutants Quantification of the Medical Effects of Air Pollution in the United Kingdom (1998)

return to text

5. Department of Health: Committee on Medical Aspects of Air Pollution Episodes Asthma and Outdoor Air Pollution (1995) paragraph 10.27

return to text

6. Whitelegg et al Traffic and Health report for Greenpeace Environmental Trust (1993)

return to text

7. Parliamentary Office of Science & Technology Breathing in our Cities (1994) paragraph 4.1.2

return to text

8. National Asthma Campaign National Asthma Audit 1996

return to text

9. Maddison, Pearce et al The True Costs of Road Transport

Document: Done

Business ▲ Tech ▲ Fun ▲ Interact ▲

UNDERSTANDING THE TEXT

1 Like many analytical texts, this website uses some difficult and specialist words. Choose some words that are unfamiliar to you, look them up in a dictionary and write down the definitions.

2 Which statistic shows how serious air pollution is in terms of causing premature deaths?

3 Look at the graph on air pollution. Which form of air pollution does road transport produce *least* of?

4 What percentage of hydrocarbons is traffic in London responsible for producing?

5 What is the technical term for 'summertime smog'?

6 Apart from air pollution, what other explanation is there for the increase in asthma cases?

INTERPRETING THE TEXT

7 **a** Find five facts in the text about air pollution.

   b How reliable does this text seem? What comments can you make about the sources of its facts?

8 Analytical texts often use a lot of facts and statistics to make their case. This text uses footnotes (small numbers in the text referring to notes at the end of the document) rather than including all the sources in the main text. Why do you think the writer has chosen to use footnotes in this way?

9 Who do you think the text is aimed at – general readers, people with a special interest in the topic, politicians, young people …? Write a sentence or two explaining who you think is the target audience.

LANGUAGE AND STRUCTURE

1 Look at the structure of the text:

> introduction
>
> ↓
>
> analysis of the problem
>
> ↓
>
> suggestions for what readers can do

Why is this structure a good one for making the text seem reliable and informative?

2 Look at the first paragraph. How does the writer use language to show how serious the problem is?

Hint

You might comment on:

- the vocabulary the writer uses
- the style of the first sentence.

---

3 Why does the writer use questions for some of the sub-headings (e.g. 'Who is at risk?')? Why are these sub-headings a useful way of linking the paragraphs together?

4 In the paragraph on people at risk, the writer starts with a statement:

The health of up to one in five people in the UK is particularly at risk from air pollution.

Look at the next sentence:

These include young children, pregnant women, the elderly, and people suffering from heart and lung diseases.

Why does the writer choose these groups of people to illustrate the point? How does it help to make the argument more persuasive?

5 The writer is careful not to express personal opinions, but sometimes quotes other people's views.

   a Write down an example where the writer integrates a quotation of other people's views into the text.

   b How does this help add authority to the writer's case?

WRITING ACTIVITY

The writer of this website analyses facts and statistics to build a case about road pollution. If you were writing a more personal opinion piece using the data, how would you express it?

Imagine you are writing a letter to a local newspaper about levels of pollution in your area. You are writing for a general audience. How will you use the information from the text and make your argument clear and powerful?

Write a two-paragraph letter, giving some facts from this text and your own opinion. You might start like this:

Dear Sir/Madam

I am writing to ask our local politicians to take road pollution more seriously …

End your letter by making recommendations for what your readers could do to help.

Unit 7
Extended writing

Write an analytical text which uses a strong base of evidence. Get hold of facts, statistics and other data to support your points, and try to convince your readers to agree with your conclusions.

You might choose one of the topics below:

1 Prison is not an effective punishment:

 ◆ Find data to show how many people are sent to prison.

 ◆ What alternative sentences could they have received?

 ◆ What are the re-offending rates of people in prison?

 ◆ What are the re-offending rates of people doing community service or under other supervision?

 ◆ What do you recommend should happen?

2 Alcohol abuse is a more serious problem than cigarettes:

 ◆ Find data about illnesses and deaths caused by alcohol and smoking.

 ◆ Look at the amount spent in hospitals treating both types of illness.

 ◆ Which creates the bigger problem?

 ◆ What would you recommend we do about it?

3 People should be encouraged to switch from cars to public transport:

 ◆ Find out how many cars there are in the UK.

 ◆ Research the amount of congestion there is.

 ◆ Investigate the costs of pollution.

 ◆ Suggest ways of getting more people to share car journeys or use trains.

Structure your essay like this:

Opening section

- Try to grab the reader's attention with a punchy opening statement.

- Set out what you believe the situation is.

- Try to make it impersonal (avoid saying I).

Developing the analysis

- Present the evidence. Use statistics, graphs, footnotes, and quotations.

- Use connectives to link ideas.

- Write in the present tense.

Conclusion

- Sum up the evidence you have presented.

- Make recommendations about what should happen.

- Address readers in the second person ('You could help by …') and suggest what they might do.

How advice texts work

Advice texts aim to give us information which helps us. They may aim to change our attitudes or behaviour, or encourage us to buy a product. They may be addressed to a particular audience, such as people of a certain age group or gender, or to a specialist audience. Advice texts may be similar to instruction texts.

An advice text may use:

- **illustrations** such as photographs and diagrams
- the **second-person** form to address the reader directly
- an **informal tone**
- a **range of sentence types** to make the text more varied, especially simple and compound sentences
- a range of **statements, questions** and **commands**
- some **description** to make the advice easier to follow
- vocabulary that is **simple** and straightforward, except where **technical terms** are needed for advice about a specialist topic.

UNIT 8

Official advice

Sun Safety

Introduction

Some advice texts have a deliberately informal tone – think of the advice columns in magazines and newspapers. But others give advice in a more impersonal way. They aim to create a sense of authority – reassuring readers that this is very solid, reliable advice.

These texts are taken from government documents. The first is from the Department of Health website, giving guidelines on avoiding too much direct sunlight. The second text is from a government website aimed at teachers. It is intended to help them teach students about important health issues.

Look at the way both texts present 'official' advice in an authoritative way. When you have studied them, you will be able to write an advice text of your own.

Text A

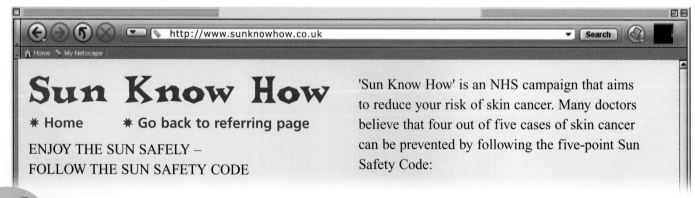

http://www.sunknowhow.co.uk Search

Home My Netscape

Sun Know How

✳ Home   ✳ Go back to referring page

ENJOY THE SUN SAFELY –
FOLLOW THE SUN SAFETY CODE

'Sun Know How' is an NHS campaign that aims to reduce your risk of skin cancer. Many doctors believe that four out of five cases of skin cancer can be prevented by following the five-point Sun Safety Code:

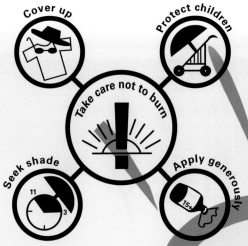

Take care not to burn

A tan may make you feel healthy, but it's a sign your skin is being damaged and it will lead to premature ageing of the skin. And you may find that you can't join in activities with friends because you're in too much pain from over-indulging in the sun!

Prolonged exposure to intense sunlight (or artificial UV radiation) can be bad for all skin colours – although people with black or brown skin have a lower risk of developing skin cancer – so take the following precautions:

* Shade your face to prevent heatstroke and eye damage
* Take care not to burn
* Shift to the shade around midday.

Are sunbeds safe?

The use of sunbeds is not encouraged as it could lead to skin damage from ultra violet (UV) radiation. You should never use a sunbed if you are under 16, have a lot of freckles or moles, burn easily, have a family history of skin cancer or are using medication that could make your skin more sensitive. Health and Safety Executive (HSE) guidance is that no one should have more than 20 sunbed sessions a year.

Cover up with loose, cool clothing, a hat and sunglasses

Seek shade during the hottest part of the day

Apply a high-factor sunscreen (SPF 15 or above) to any parts of your body exposed to the sun

What does SPF mean?

The SPF, or Sun Protection Factor, is a measure of how much a sunscreen protects your skin. The higher the SPF, the greater the protection. It is measured by timing how long skin covered with sunscreen takes to burn compared with unprotected skin. So, if your skin would burn in 10 minutes in the midday sun, using an SPF of two would double the time spent before burning to 20 minutes. However, you should use sunscreens to give yourself greater protection rather than to stay in the sun for longer.

Which SPF should I choose?

Choose an SPF with a factor of 15 or over. But limit the amount of time you spend in the sun, too. Don't forget to apply it thickly over all exposed areas and re-apply regularly, especially after swimming. Remember areas such as ears, neck, hands, feet and bald patch!

Text B

www.sunsafety.co.uk | Search

Home | My Netscape

About   Search   HOME   Links   Feedback

Facts
Schools &
Curriculum
Links

Sun Safety

Introduction

The increasing incidence of skin cancer in Britain is an issue that affects parents and schools.

There are more than 50,000 new cases of skin cancer and 2,000 deaths from skin cancer each year. Skin cancer is almost always caused by the sun. The increasing incidence of skin cancer in Britain is an issue that affects parents and schools. Prolonged over-exposure to the sun and episodes of sunburn under the age of 15 are major risk factors for skin cancer later in life. The British Association of Dermatology estimates that four out of five skin cancer deaths are preventable.

Sun awareness is a safety issue, and schools will want to prevent the possibility of sunburn while pupils are at school or on school trips. The best approach is one that combines:

✪ Education about sun safety. Learning should include knowledge about the sun, its effects on the environment and human life, the risk of skin cancer and ways to protect ourselves.

✪ Protection from the sun. Practical protection in the form of shade and appropriate clothing and high-factor sunscreen (SPF15+) is the most effective way of preventing sunburn and reducing the risk of skin cancer.

When discussing sun safety, remember that moderate exposure to summer sunshine is essential for our bodies to produce the required amount of vitamin D. This vitamin is very important in building and maintaining healthy bones.

Return to MAIN MENU

Document: Done

Business ✦ Tech ✦ Fun ✦ Interact ✦

UNDERSTANDING THE TEXT

Text A

1 What is a suntan a sign of?

2 The text asks the question: 'Are sunbeds safe?' What is the answer?

3 What does HSE stand for?

4 Which SPF are you advised to choose?

Text B

5 What proportion of skin cancer deaths cannot be prevented?

6 What two roles should teachers perform, according to the text?

7 Why do our bodies need some exposure to the sun?

INTERPRETING THE TEXT

8 Advice texts are usually addressed to a particular audience. How can you tell that Text B is aimed chiefly at teachers?

9 Both texts appear on official websites.

a Which text feels more personal or friendly? Try to explain why.

b Do both texts seem reliable as a source of facts? Explain why or why not.

10 a How do these websites differ from printed texts – what features do they have that you wouldn't include on paper?

b Which one do you think makes better use of the possibilities of ICT (information and communication technology)? Explain your response.

LANGUAGE AND STRUCTURE

1 Like many advice texts, Text A uses the second-person form.

   a Write down an example of a sentence from the text using the second person.

   b What effect does this have?

2 Text B uses the third person, rather than addressing readers directly as 'you'. What effect does this have?

3 Advice texts often use technical terms. Both of these texts use the term 'SPF'. Text A explains what SPF means but Text B uses the term without explaining it. What does this tell you about the audience it is aimed at?

4 Look at these two sentences from Text A:

And you may find that you can't join in activities with friends because you're in too much pain from over-indulging in the sun!

Remember areas such as ears, neck, hands, feet and bald patch!

Why does the writer use exclamation marks? What is the effect of using these?

5 Text B uses quite formal language in places. Look at this phrase:

prolonged over-exposure to the sun

How might the same idea be expressed in a less formal way? Write down an informal version of the phrase.

6 Advice texts often use statements, questions and commands.

   a Find an example of each of these types of sentence in Text A.

   b Does Text B use all of these sentence functions?

WRITING ACTIVITY

Both texts use quite formal language. Imagine you were giving some hints to a friend after learning about the potential risks of sunbathing. How would you express your ideas in order to make your advice effective?

Imagine a conversation, and write down what you might say. Try to persuade your friend that he or she must be careful.

Then use arrows and labels to show which parts of your language are different from a formal, written, official text. You might start like this:

second-person form – suggests a one-to-one conversation

informal opening phrase

You know, you've really got to be careful when you're spending much time in the sun. It's a lot more dangerous than it seems …

contracted verb form shows informality

Unit 8

Extended writing

Your task is to create an authoritative website on an important issue. Aim to give readers useful and convincing advice.

You might choose one of these topics:

- How to revise effectively
- How to care for a certain type of pet
- How to maintain a mountain bike
- How to improve your diet and exercise patterns

Remember: the challenge is to create a website and, even though you will probably be working on paper, you need to think about the features and potential of ICT. You should include:

- ideas for graphics and animations that will make the message fun and more easy to follow
- layout features that are easy to navigate
- hypertext links so that readers can move between different screens to get the information they need
- interactive features (e.g. self-assessment quizzes and tests).

To be authoritative you need to use a fairly serious (but not stuffy) tone, and combine facts with advice.

Remember to:

- use the present tense
- use the second person to address the reader directly
- use the third person for impersonal effect where appropriate
- use statements, questions and commands
- use a variety of sentences
- keep paragraphs very short
- use a glossary to explain technical terms.

When you have written your text, review it with a partner. Decide what you have written well, and which passages could be improved. Which writing skills do you still need to develop?

How reviews work

The purpose of a review is to analyse something, comment on it and show its strengths and weaknesses. Reviews are often written of books, plays and films. They will usually contain **analysis** (an account of the features the reviewer notices), plus a **judgement** (what the reviewer thinks of its quality).

A review will usually be structured as a **logical argument**, discussing one point at a time, supporting each with **evidence** (such as a quotation). A review may conclude with the writer's personal **opinion** or a **summary** of the points made.

A review will often:

◆ use the **third person** for an impersonal style

◆ be written in the **present tense**

◆ use **connectives** to link points together in a logical way, such as *however, as a result, this means that*

◆ use **technical terms** related to the subject discussed

◆ include vocabulary related to **comment** when giving the writer's opinions.

Writing about texts

Not Waving but Drowning

Learning objectives

This unit contains a poem and a review of the poem, written in the form of an essay. You will be studying the following objectives:

- Word level: use terms for analysing language; explore the use of connectives

- Sentence level: review and develop complex sentences in your own writing; integrate speech, reference and quotation into your writing

- Reading: explore the use of rhetorical devices

- Writing: offer advice in an impersonal style; present a balanced analysis; support your opinions of a text with evidence

Introduction

When you write about literature, the idea is to show your response to the text, not just say what it is about or what happens in it. This means balancing analysis (what you notice) with judgement (what you think of it).

Here is a poem to read, followed by a brief essay commenting upon it. Notice the way the writer of the essay makes judgements about the text and supports them with examples. When you have studied this review, you can write one of your own.

Not waving but drowning

Nobody heard him, the dead man,
But still he lay moaning:
I was much further out than you thought
And not waving but drowning.

Poor chap, he always loved larking
And now he's dead.
It must have been too cold for him his heart gave way,
They said.

Oh, no no no, it was too cold always
(Still the dead one lay moaning)
I was much too far out all my life
And not waving but drowning.

Stevie Smith

UNDERSTANDING THE TEXT

1 What has happened to the man in the first stanza?

2 What did people watching him think he was doing?

3 Look at the second stanza: what is the reaction of people to his death?

4 What do you think the man means in the final stanza when he says 'I was much too far out all my life / And not waving but drowning'?

Now read this response to the poem.

'Not Waving but Drowning'

The poem by Stevie Smith has a dramatic, unexpected title which immediately catches our attention. It makes us wonder what the poem will be about. The first line then helps us to make sense of the title. We realize it is about a 'dead man'.

The poem is confusing at first because it keeps changing point of view. The first two lines are written from the viewpoint of someone who sees the drowning man, perhaps from the shore. We are detached from him and the writer refers to the man as 'he'. Suddenly in the third line we are

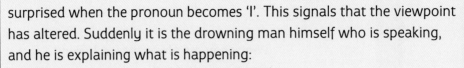

surprised when the pronoun becomes 'I'. This signals that the viewpoint has altered. Suddenly it is the drowning man himself who is speaking, and he is explaining what is happening:

I was much further out than you thought

And not waving but drowning.

The dead man is addressing us directly, referring to us as 'you', as if we are the people on the beach who misunderstood his movements. There is something quite shocking about this – first, that the dead man is speaking to us, and second that the people on shore have let him die without realizing that he was in trouble.

The next section – stanza two – returns to the point of view of the spectators. This time they are looking back on their memories of the drowned man: 'it must have been too cold for him'. The writer uses understatement here – 'poor chap' – to suggest that the people on shore are not very upset. They describe the man's death in a very matter-of-fact way.

The last stanza returns to the viewpoint of the drowned man. It is like a reply to the spectators' words in the previous stanza. He explains that 'I was much too far out all my life'. I think by this the narrator means that he feels he was always out of his depth. He spent his life struggling to cope and asking for help. People always misunderstood him. They thought he was 'waving' when in fact he was 'drowning'.

The poem shows us how easy it can be to misunderstand people, to assume that their surface appearance is what they are like beneath. The poem also illustrates how difficult modern life can be, where everyone struggles to stay afloat, and few people really understand you. It is quite a disturbing poem, and more complex than the simple storyline at first appears.

INTERPRETING THE TEXT

5 The essay starts by commenting on the title. Why is this a good starting point?

6 The reviewer describes features of the poem – such as the shifting viewpoint – and also makes judgements about their effects, such as saying 'The poem is confusing at first'.

a Write down an example of a statement or description

b Write down an example of a judgement or evaluation.

7 Do you think the writer gets the balance right between describing what he or she notices and giving opinions – or would you have done it differently?

8 Review writers should use evidence to back up their arguments. How well do you think this writer uses quotations as evidence?

a Are there enough of them in the essay? Are they too long or too short?

b Are they used skilfully to explain the text to the reader?

9 The reviewer does not comment on the poem's rhyme scheme, or the structure of its stanzas. Write down one point the writer could have made about these.

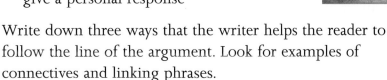

LANGUAGE AND STRUCTURE

1 The structure of the essay is:

introduce the text

↓

analyse the text

↓

give a personal response

Write down three ways that the writer helps the reader to follow the line of the argument. Look for examples of connectives and linking phrases.

2 The writer uses evidence from the text in two ways: by using separate quotations, and by building quotations into sentences.

a How does the writer set out the separate quotation to make it clear to the reader? Comment on the use of layout and punctuation.

b Choose an example where the writer builds a quotation into a sentence, and describe how this works.

3 Although the review is analytical, the writing is quite personal. Sometimes the writer uses 'we' and later 'I'. How effective do you find this use of the first-person style? Would the essay be better if it seemed more impersonal?

4 Look at the writer's sentence style in the first paragraph of the essay:

The poem by Stevie Smith has a dramatic, unexpected title which immediately catches our attention. (1) It makes us wonder what the poem will be about. (2) The first line then helps us to make sense of the title. (3) We realize it is about a 'dead man'. (4)

All of these are complex sentences, but sentences 2, 3 and 4 are all of similar length. Does this make the style seem a bit dull, and too much like a list of points? Try using a conjunction (e.g. *and*) to join sentences 3 and 4 together. Does this help to give variety?

Stevie Smith

WRITING ACTIVITY

What is your overall judgement of the essay? What do you like about it? What could be improved? Write a review of it, as if you were this student's teacher giving detailed feedback. You might comment upon:

- the structure of the essay
- the way the ideas are explained
- the use of quotations
- the vocabulary used
- the sentence structures
- the balance of description and review.

Try to give as much specific feedback as possible. Aim to balance positive comments with suggestions about areas that could be developed.

Unit 9 Extended writing

Read this poem by Frances Cornford. Then write a personal response to it, like the essay on pages 97 to 98. The questions below may help you to explore the poem.

A Recollection

My father's friend came once to tea.

He laughed and talked. He spoke to me.

But in another week they said

That friendly pink-faced man was dead.

'How sad …' they said, 'the best of men . . .'

So I said, too, 'How sad'; but then

Deep in my heart I thought, with pride,

'I know a person who has died'.

Frances Cornford

Frances Cornford

1 What do we learn about the character of the narrator?

2 Where and when do you think the poem is set?

3 How can we tell that the narrator is a child? How does the writer emphasize this?

4 Why does the narrator imitate the comments of the adults?

5 What is the poem telling us about childhood views of death?

Writing about the text

A Write an opening statement saying what the poem is about.

B Next, analyse the poem in sequence, following its development line by line. Aim to comment on the language used, what happens, what we learn about the setting, and what the narrator is like.

C Conclude by summing up what the poem shows us about the narrator, and what it shows about the way children view death.

   ◆ Use an analytical style, perhaps using *we* and I when necessary.

   ◆ Use both separate and embedded quotations to support your comments.

   ◆ Aim to use a variety of sentence lengths.

D When you have finished, discuss your work with a partner. Which parts of your review are most effective? Which skills do you need to develop further for writing about poetry?

Assess Your Learning

Unit 6 Persuasive writing

Think back to the debate about traffic that you participated in for the speaking and listening assignment on page 76.

Below is a list of speaking and listening skills that you should have displayed during the debate. Review your performance by putting them in order of how well you feel you did. First on the list should be what you feel you did best. Last on the list should be what you feel you most need to work on.

- Working together
- Listening carefully
- Getting your views across
- Using appropriate language
- Using Standard English

Unit 7 Analytical writing

1 Look at the analytical text you produced for the extended writing task on pages 85 to 86. Copy and complete the chart to evaluate how well you achieved your aims at the different stages.

Opening section	Yes/no	Example
Did you grab the reader's attention?		
Did you set out what the situation is?		
Did you keep the style impersonal?		
Developing the analysis		
Did you use supporting evidence?		
Which connectives did you use to link ideas?		
Did you use the present tense?		
Conclusion		
Did you sum up the evidence you presented?		
Did you make recommendations about what should happen?		
Did you address the reader in the second person?		

2 What are the main areas of your analytical writing you now need to develop?

Unit 8 Advice texts

With a partner, evaluate your skills in reading website advice texts.

1 Copy the chart and explain what the reader needs to do for each skill.

Reading skills for website advice texts	How I do this	My progress
Identify the audience the text is aimed at		○
Work out how reliable a text is		○
Judge how well a text makes use of website features		○
Understand the effect of the writer's choice of language		○

2 Decide with your partner which traffic light best matches your progress so far and colour it in the chart.

● I find this difficult.

◐ I'm doing quite well at this, but not all the time.

○ I'm doing well at this.

Unit 9 Reviews

Look at the poetry review you wrote for the extended writing task on pages 101 to 102.

1 Ask a partner to read through your work and in the margin use the following codes to highlight some key features:

O – opening statement saying what the poem is about

A – analytical style (only using 'I' and 'we' when necessary)

EQ – use of embedded quotations within your own sentences

SQ – use of separate quotations to support your comments

SV – sentence variety; note examples of three different-length sentences

2 Look at the notes your partner has made. If you were marking your own assignment, what would you say were:

- its strengths
- areas for development?

Imagine, Explore, Entertain

Getting started

Unit 10 Narrative and structure

In a multiple narration, a story is told by more than one person or character. Explore this technique with a partner. Together, choose a story you know well, such as *Little Red Riding Hood*.

Tell the story – but each of you tell it from a different point of view. For example:

Partner 1: *Once upon a time there was a little girl called Little Red Riding Hood.*
Partner 2: *There was also a wolf.*
Partner 1: *Little Red Riding Hood woke up one beautiful day. She had never felt happier.*
Partner 2: *The wolf woke up in his lair one day. He had never felt hungrier …*

Unit 11 Non-fiction texts

Look at the mystery texts below.

◆ What clues are there in each text that indicate it might be fiction or non-fiction?

◆ What type of text might it be (e.g. history, autobiography, travel writing, journalism)?

Be prepared to justify your ideas with evidence from the texts.

> **A** At 2 or 3 or 4 am, somewhere along in there, on August 25, 1966, his forty-eighth birthday, in fact, Leonard Bernstein woke up in the dark in a state of wild alarm.

> **B** I went to Lippington when I was eight. My first few weeks were as miserable as I expected them to be.

> **C** It was snowing in Litewska Street; not big heavy flakes but small, hard, blinding droplets, almost sleet, that blessed the dull suburban road with a kind of grey fog.

> **D** Captain George Manby had reached the age of forty without having contributed significantly to life.

> **E** The boulevard du Cange was a broad, quiet street that marked the eastern flank of the city of Amiens.

Unit 12 Poetic forms and styles

Read the list of features below. Rank them in order of importance in poetry. (Be prepared to justify the order that you choose.)

- vivid images
- emotional content
- unusual vocabulary
- rhythm
- rhyme
- a message or moral

Unit 13 Writers from different times

A 'thriller' is an exciting story, often about crime or violence, which grabs the audience's attention and holds it right to the end.

Here is a bad opening of a thriller:

It was really dark. There was a lot of fog creeping in from the graveyard like a cat. Clouds covered the full moon and someone in a dark coat was standing under a tree. He looked really creepy.

Working with a partner, create a new version that would make us want to read on. Be prepared to explain how you have heightened the sense of mystery and suspense.

Unit 14 Drama scripts

Here are two extracts of spoken English: one is unscripted, from a racing commentary; the other is from a play.

Unscripted speech	Scripted speech
Away they break then (.) er *Jelba* one of the last to break sits at the back of the field along with er *Karasta* who er has yet to settle (.) she's running very freely out the back and Johnny Murtagh will er in fact she hasn't settled at all …	**A:** I remember that day at the races. **B:** What do you mean? **A:** You know – that day at Newmarket, the day it all went so badly wrong. *Pause* **B:** I don't know what you're talking about.

Use the extracts to decide on the three main features of a) scripted speech, and b) unscripted speech.

Unit 15 Cultural context

In English, as in many other languages, there are stories that have had a powerful influence on our culture. For example: King Arthur; Hercules; Noah's Ark; Beauty and the Beast.

Jot down two arguments for and two arguments against teaching these stories in schools.

Multiple narration

A Lesson

Learning objectives

These are the objectives you will be studying:

- Word level: recognize layers of meaning

- Sentence level: develop your paragraphing skills

- Reading: explore the use of rhetorical devices

- Writing: explore narrative techniques; support your opinions of a text with evidence

- Speaking and listening: compare points of view; evaluate evidence to reach a considered viewpoint

Introduction

Stories are often structured so that they have more than one storyline. Think of films and television dramas; in most soap operas the average length of a scene will be less than 15 seconds, then we will switch to other characters in a different setting. In this way, the writer can push the story forward by constantly moving between different groups of characters.

Fiction writers often use this technique, especially when they wish to build suspense. The key moments of the novel *Jaws*, for example, switch rapidly between the 'big fish' out at sea and the victim swimming in the water.

One paragraph focuses on the shark, the next on the boy, then the shark again, as the writer gradually draws the two storylines together. This is known as **multiple narration**.

This unit looks at a complete short story, which is told through the use of two narratives. Elizabeth Garner's story is confusing at first and difficult to follow. She makes the reader work hard to follow what is being described. Suddenly it becomes clearer, once we understand how the two storylines connect.

A Lesson

He was trying to teach them Geography — or so he said. He drew on the globe a black dot. It marked a town in Australia.

The town on the other side of the world plunged into darkness. No match would strike. No fire could burn. In terrified blindness they all reached for the modern reassurance of electricity. The switches gave nothing. Together they rushed to their television sets and turned them on.

Blank.

There was nothing; not even a dancing fog of black and white dots. Only a silent, menacing darkness.

They tried to tune their radios to hear some sound other than their own.

Silence.

The speakers hissed at them.

They thought that it was the end of the world.

He was trying to teach them Geography — or so he said. He spun the globe faster and faster.

Words which marked time were soon forgotten. Lifetimes dwindled to a passing moment.

Their suffering did not last long. They became accustomed to the dark silence which grew over them. They each held their own dark close.

He stopped the globe.

Time waited for him.

He wiped the black dot clean and placed the globe on the table.

On the other side of the world the sun shone through the town. The radios spewed loud music. Brightly-coloured figures leered at them from their television screens. These sudden noises attacked them all. They felt it was the end of their world.

He looked up and saw that the classroom was empty. He thought it was some childish prank. He stood up sharply, in his anger knocking over the globe. It fell and shattered into a thousand pieces.

Elizabeth Garner

UNDERSTANDING THE TEXT

1 What does the teacher do?

2 What is the effect of his action?

3 How do the people on the other side of the world react?

4 Why does the teacher get angry at the end of the story?

INTERPRETING THE TEXT

5 What impression do you get of the teacher in the story? What hints are there that he is not entirely good or trustworthy?

6 How does the writer make the people seem helpless and panicky?

7 How can you tell that there is a link between what the teacher does and what happens across the world?

8 What do you think is the writer's 'message' in the story?

 ◆ Is she suggesting something about the link between what we do on this side of the world and its impact elsewhere?

 ◆ Is she showing us someone who is evil?

 ◆ Is she simply writing a supernatural story?

 Explain your ideas.

9 Why do you think the story is called 'A Lesson'?

LANGUAGE AND STRUCTURE

1 **a** One rhetorical device in this story is the author's use of pronouns. Look at the first paragraph. The writer refers to the teacher as 'he' rather than giving him a name. What effect does this have?

 b Look at the second paragraph. Why does the writer call the people 'they' and avoid giving names, or any descriptive detail?

2 The writer sometimes uses very short paragraphs, like this:

Blank.

Silence.

Why do you think she structures them like this?

3 The writer uses a dual narrative to tell her story. Why do you think she does this? Write a couple of sentences to explain how the dual narrative increases the tension in the story.

4 Read this comment on the story:

The writer makes us dislike the teacher. She wants us to feel that he is untrustworthy, even evil.

In a small group, discuss whether you agree with this statement. What evidence can you find in the story to support it? Try to reach agreement in your group. Make notes of your findings and your evidence, and report back to the class.

WRITING ACTIVITY

How could you make the teacher in the opening paragraph a more sympathetic (likeable) character? Would it have an impact if he:

♦ was given a name

♦ was described in greater detail

♦ was given some dialogue?

Try writing an opening paragraph in which you aim to show that the teacher is a trustworthy, likeable character who is simply doing his job.

You might start like this:

'Morning everyone,' said Mr ...

Then write a paragraph explaining how you approached the task.

Extended writing

Here is the outline of a story:

A child is digging in the garden. Suddenly the child finds something he or she doesn't recognize. The child digs harder, and then looks closely – it's flesh of some kind, grey and thick. Suddenly it moves. The earth starts to shift. A baby dinosaur starts to scramble out of the earth. The child is first terrified, and then delighted.

Write three versions of the opening paragraphs of this story using the narrative devices below:

A	B	C
Open the story with the child digging.	Open the story with the leg moving, and something pushing through the soil.	Open with the dinosaur lying beneath the earth.
Tell the story in chronological order.	Cut to the child's mother watching from the kitchen window. She sees something is going on and rushes out.	Tell the story from the dinosaur's point of view, like this: 'I had lain there, beneath that dusty soil, for as long as I could remember …'
Tell it in the third person ('he' or 'she')	Cut to the child, panic stricken.	Then cut to the child on the surface just about to start digging.
	Cut to the mother running out to help.	

When you have finished, decide which version works best. Write a few sentences to explain why.

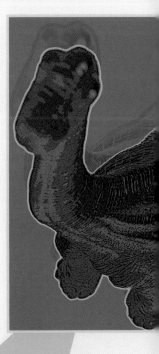

Conveying ideas

11

Walking on Water

Learning objectives

You will be studying the following objectives:

- Word level: recognize layers of meaning

- Sentence level: vary the formality of your writing; investigate the organization and conventions of websites

- Reading: gather information from a range of sources; compare the way ideas, values or emotions are presented; comment on different interpretations; explore the use of rhetorical devices

- Writing: use language creatively; explore how information texts can be entertaining; integrate varied information into a single account

Introduction

Non-fiction writers sometimes use the techniques we expect of poets and novelists. They might use figurative language (e.g. similes, metaphors and personification), or sentence structure to capture our attention.

In this unit you will compare two non-fiction texts. The first text is an example of sports writing, and it combines autobiography with storytelling. It describes Andy Martin's first time surfing on a fashionable Quigly surfboard. The second text is from a website belonging to the University of San Diego, California. It gives hints on surfing.

Comparing the two texts should help you to see the difference between literary non-fiction and straight non-fiction writing.

Text A

The writer, Andy Martin, has lent a pair of eye-catching socks to his friend, Louis. In return, he gets to borrow Louis's state-of-the-art surfboard …

Glossary

implacable – *determined*

chronometrically – *according to a clock*

Walking on Water

Louis had a beautiful board. It was a remake of a classic 60s malibu: nine feet long, broad in the hip, but light, with a rounded nose and three fins, in deep blue with orange stripes and a crimson rim. It bore the signature of Quigly, a West Coast shaper who had been prominent in the revival of the longboard in the eighties.

I lusted after that Quigly. Thus it was that when Louis wondered if there was anything he could do for me in return for the socks, I mentioned I was currently without a board.

'You want to borrow my Quigly?' he said. It was more a plea than a question. Unscrambled, his message read: 'Please don't take my Quigly! It's the love of my life.'

I was implacable. 'If you can spare it for a few hours,' I said.

'Have you surfed much on the North Shore?' he inquired.

'Sure,' I said, truthfully. 'Jocko's, Freddie's, Haleiwa, Lani's, Backyards. All over.' I passed over the details of what had taken place.

'Oh well, I guess that's all right, then.' He sounded reassured.

The following morning I steered the Quigly into the car like a kidnap victim and headed for Haleiwa. Bodo and Damon were waiting for me.

'That's a fine board you have there,' said Bodo.

'A Quigly,' I boasted.

'Wow!' gasped Damon. 'They're like gold dust in California.'

I had a good feeling about that board. It felt right as I gave it a solid basting of wax and uncurled the leash, and it felt right as I paddled it out: well balanced, smooth through the water, responsive. Bodo called it a 'modern tanker': it was a subtle compromise between a gondola and a toothpick, combining the virtues of robustness and sensitivity, stability and speed.

I followed Bodo and Damon out through the channel. The Quigly sliced through the oncoming waves like a knife through butter, so by the time we hit the line-up I was still in good shape. There was a right-hander and further over towards the harbour a left. We opted for the left, which was less crowded. Bodo and Damon drove straight at the peak. But I didn't want to push my luck and followed my usual cautious procedure of testing out the unoccupied shoulder.

I lined myself up with an easygoing four- to five-footer as it ambled into shore, despised by the hunters further out who were stalking bigger game. I got into gear and rammed the Quigly ahead of the swell. Then I felt the wave hook itself under the rear and start to jack it up. I cranked out another couple of strokes and leapt to my feet.

It was almost too easy. It was like riding a bicycle successfully for the first time: you can't understand why you had so much difficulty before, just as before it was impossible to understand how the deed could ever be done. My feet were planted in the textbook position: my left foot halfway up the board, sideways on but angled towards the nose, my right foot slanted across the board at the tail. Surprised to find myself still upright, I flung out my arms and crouched, modelling myself on the famous picture of Eddie Aikau. The Quigly planed down the face and, almost without my exerting any effort, began to curve into a leisurely bottom turn. Behind me and to the right, the wave was bursting apart: over my left shoulder was an unbroken section. I leaned over, slid my weight onto my right foot, and the Quigly carved a voluptuous line along the crystal-blue wall, like Michelangelo shaping his Madonna. I had no idea how long I'd been standing up. Chronometrically, it would be insignificant; but I have a mental clock permanently arrested with its hands on that morning and that wave. 'No one times how long the ride is,' Mark Foo had said to me. 'It's so intense, the duration doesn't matter. A second is a long time on the wave.'

Andy Martin

Text B

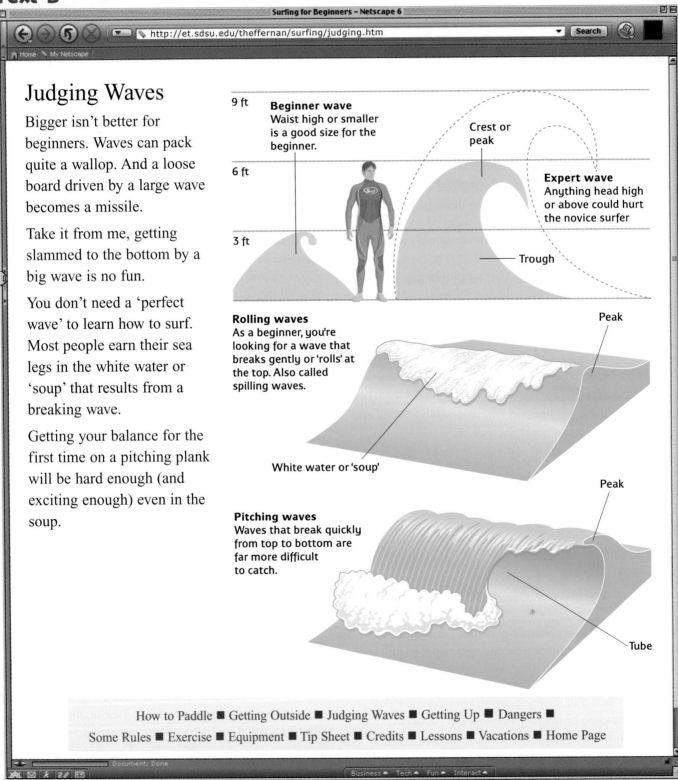

Surfing for Beginners – Netscape 6

http://et.sdsu.edu/theffernan/surfing/judging.htm

Home My Netscape

Judging Waves

Bigger isn't better for beginners. Waves can pack quite a wallop. And a loose board driven by a large wave becomes a missile.

Take it from me, getting slammed to the bottom by a big wave is no fun.

You don't need a 'perfect wave' to learn how to surf. Most people earn their sea legs in the white water or 'soup' that results from a breaking wave.

Getting your balance for the first time on a pitching plank will be hard enough (and exciting enough) even in the soup.

9 ft

6 ft

3 ft

Beginner wave
Waist high or smaller is a good size for the beginner.

Crest or peak

Expert wave
Anything head high or above could hurt the novice surfer

Trough

Rolling waves
As a beginner, you're looking for a wave that breaks gently or 'rolls' at the top. Also called spilling waves.

Peak

White water or 'soup'

Pitching waves
Waves that break quickly from top to bottom are far more difficult to catch.

Peak

Tube

How to Paddle ■ Getting Outside ■ Judging Waves ■ Getting Up ■ Dangers ■
Some Rules ■ Exercise ■ Equipment ■ Tip Sheet ■ Credits ■ Lessons ■ Vacations ■ Home Page

Documents Done

Business Tech Fun Interact

Surfing for Beginners - Netscape 6

◁ ▷ ↻ ✕ ▽ 🔖 http://et.sdsu.edu/theffernan/surfing/tip_sheet.htm ▾ **Search**

🏠 Home ✎ My Netscape

Beginner's Tip Sheet

To help remember what you need to do when that awesome wave is coming, print out this page. Next, trim it with scissors to match the nose of your surfboard, then tape it down with two-inch-wide clear packing tape. Be sure to cover the entire paper with tape. Now, let's go surfing!

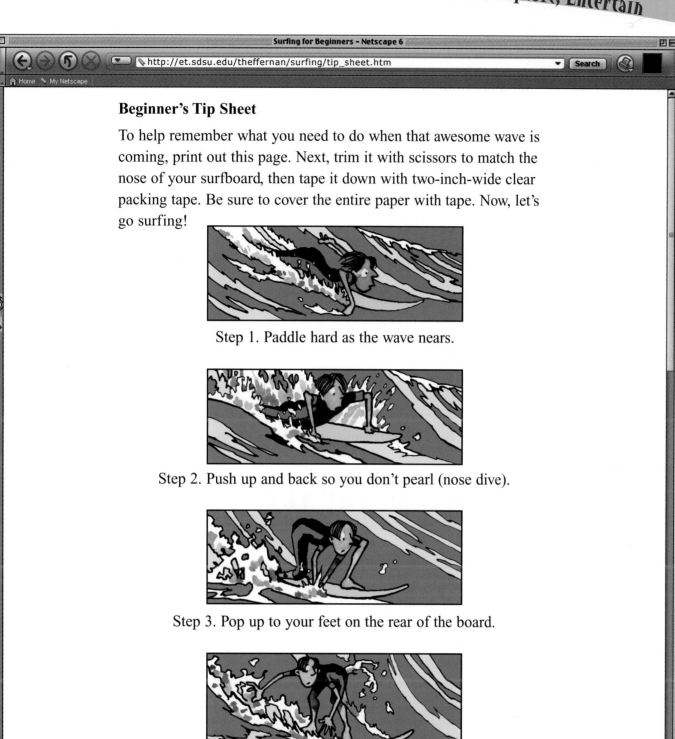

Step 1. Paddle hard as the wave nears.

Step 2. Push up and back so you don't pearl (nose dive).

Step 3. Pop up to your feet on the rear of the board.

Step 4. Stay low, get your balance and begin a leaning turn.

If you fell, try again. Be persistent and you'll get there.

How to Paddle ■ Getting Outside ■ Judging Waves ■ Getting Up ■ Dangers ■
Some Rules ■ Exercise ■ Equipment ■ Tip Sheet ■ Credits ■ Lessons ■ Vacations ■ Home Page

Document: Done

Business▲ Tech▲ Fun▲ Interact▲

Text A

1 Why is the surfboard called a Quigly?

2 Does Louis really want the narrator to borrow his board? How can you tell?

3 How does the writer get the board ready before going out to sea?

4 How can you tell that the Quigly performs well in the water?

5 What point does the writer make about time at the end of the extract?

Text B

6 In surfing, what does the word 'soup' mean?

7 What is another term for rolling waves?

8 Name two dangers for beginners that the writer mentions.

INTERPRETING THE TEXT

Text A

9 How does the writer make the Quigly surfboard seem glamorous and exciting?

> # Hint
>
> Look at:
>
> • the way he describes it
>
> • how other people react to it
>
> • the writer's own feelings about it.

10 How can you tell that the new surfboard makes surfing easier than the writer expected?

Text B

11 How does the writer reassure readers that, with practice, they will become successful surfers?

12 a How useful do you find the diagrams in this text? Do they help explain how to surf? Are they more or less informative than the words beside them?

b Write a sentence or two to describe the ways you extracted information from this text to answer the questions – did the diagrams and labels help you?

13 This text comes from a website. How would you know that if you had not been told? Are there any clues in the text that show it is from the Internet?

Comparison

14 How would you describe the purpose and audience of the two texts?

15 Which text makes surfing seem more exciting? Explain why.

LANGUAGE AND STRUCTURE

Text A

1 In the first paragraph, the writer describes the Quigly surfboard as having a 'hip', a 'nose' and 'fins'. What is the effect of this use of familiar words?

2 One rhetorical device the writer uses is vivid figurative language. Say in your own words what you think he means in each of these sentences:

a *It was a subtle compromise between a gondola and a toothpick.*

b *The Quigly carved a voluptuous line along the crystal-blue wall, like Michelangelo shaping his Madonna.*

c *I have a mental clock permanently arrested with its hands on that morning and that wave.*

3 Look at another of his descriptions using figurative language:

I lined myself up with an easygoing four- to five-footer as it ambled into shore, despised by the hunters further out who were stalking bigger game.

a What is he referring to when he says:

  i four- to five-footer

  ii the hunters further out

  iii bigger game?

b The language here uses metaphor, comparing one object with another to help the reader visualize it. How does the choice of metaphor capture the excitement of the waves?

Text B

4 Look at the first paragraph of the text. The writer says: 'Waves can pack quite a wallop'. If the text were written in a more formal way, how might the writer have expressed the same idea?

5 The writer's next sentence begins with 'And'. Many writers avoid starting with a conjunction like this. Why do you think this writer does so?

6 The writer uses the second-person form to address the reader directly – for example:

You don't need a 'perfect wave' ...
Getting your balance for the first time ...

How do you, as a reader, react to the writer? Does he seem:

expert arrogant reassuring helpful big-headed self-confident enthusiastic?

Choose the one word which you think best describes his tone. Explain your response with examples from the text.

WRITING ACTIVITY

Text A captures the excitement of surfing using vivid language. How would a more factual report present the same material?

Write a one-paragraph factual report of Andy Martin's experience, to appear in a local newspaper or magazine. Simply give the facts about the board he is using, and how he rides the board. Write it in the third person:

Andy Martin borrowed a Quigly surfboard from ...

Unit 11 Extended writing

The Internet is a means of giving information to readers in an entertaining, interactive way. Web pages can use text and images, plus music, animations and video.

Choose a topic you know a lot about. Some possibilities are given below. Then design a website which combines information with entertainment.

Think about how you can make the information as attractive and useful as possible. Think also about your audience. How will you choose your language and layout?

You might:

◆ use short blocks of text

◆ use sub-headings and bullet points to make text clearer

◆ build in an interactive quiz

◆ include hyperlinks to other pages

◆ use images and animations.

Possible topics

◆ How to skateboard

◆ How to download an MP3 file

◆ How to make the tastiest sandwich

◆ How to edit a digital movie

◆ How to improve the look of a word-processed document (using font styles, sizes, bold, underline, etc.)

Remember that the aim is to communicate information in an entertaining way.

Use a sheet of A4 paper to draft the website. For images, animations and movies, simply label them on the page (you don't have to draw them).

Speaking and listening:
special assignment

Learning objectives

This special assignment gives you the chance to practise interviewing. These are the objectives you will be studying:

- Speaking: reflect on how your speaking skills are developing; develop interview techniques
- Listening: reflect on your listening skills

Imagine a TV or radio reporter interviews Andy Martin about his first ride on the Quigly. What would the reporter ask? What kind of questions would draw the best answers from Andy Martin? How could the reporter avoid questions that lead to yes/no responses?

Think about your interview questions and then, in pairs, hold a two-minute interview. Swap roles, and do the interview again.

When you have finished, write a few sentences to describe what you have learned about interviewing. Which speaking and listening skills do you need to improve for future interview sessions?

Nineteenth-century poetry

Introduction

This unit looks at two poets, one from the USA who wrote in the nineteenth century; the other from Ireland who is one of the world's most admired poets today. The two poets are Emily Dickinson and Seamus Heaney.

There's Been a Death

Learning objectives

You will be studying the following objectives:

- Word level: recognize layers of meaning
- Sentence level: use the full range of punctuation to clarify meaning
- Reading: compare the way ideas, values or emotions are presented; explore the use of rhetorical devices
- Writing: use descriptive detail

Emily Dickinson is one of America's most unusual poets. Born in 1830, she spent most of the later years of her life confined to her home – refusing to leave the house. She wrote a huge amount, producing around 2,000 poems, and yet only around seven of them were published while she was alive, and they were considered deeply odd.

Her poems describe her thoughts and feelings, often about love, death and religion. She has a very individual style, which upset some of her early readers. For example, she used punctuation in an unexpected way, as you will see when you look at her poem. It is presented here in two different versions. The first is the original version, with the punctuation as Dickinson intended it. The second is a modern, edited version, which aims to standardize her punctuation to make it less 'wacky'. See how the different versions read.

The poem is on one of Dickinson's constant themes. She describes the effects of a death which has happened across the street.

Glossary

milliner – *person who makes or sells hats*

intuition – *impression*

Version A

There's been a Death, in the Opposite House,
As lately as Today –
I know it, by the numb look
Such Houses have – alway –

The Neighbours rustle in and out –
The Doctor – drives away –
A Window opens like a Pod –
Abrupt – mechanically –

Somebody flings a Mattress out –
The Children hurry by –
They wonder if it died – on that –
I used to – when a Boy –

The Minister – goes stiffly in –
As if the House were His –
And He owned all the Mourners – now –
And little Boys – besides –

And then the Milliner – and the Man
Of the Appalling Trade –
To take the measure of the House –
There'll be that Dark Parade –

Of Tassels – and of Coaches – soon –
It's easy as a Sign –
The Intuition of the News –
In just a Country Town –

Version B

There's been a death in the opposite house
As lately as today.
I know it by the numb look
Such houses have alway.

The neighbours rustle in and out;
The doctor drives away.
A window opens like a pod,
Abrupt, mechanically;

Somebody flings a mattress out.
The children hurry by;
They wonder if it died on that.
I used to, when a boy.

The minister goes stiffly in
As if the house were his
And he owned all the mourners now,
And little boys besides;

And then the milliner, and the man
Of the appalling trade
To take the measure of the house.
There'll be that dark parade

Of tassels and of coaches soon.
It's easy as a sign —
The intuition of the news
In just a country town.

Emily Dickinson

UNDERSTANDING THE TEXT

1 Look at the first stanza of Versions A and B. Write down two differences you notice in their layout.

2 Following the death at the house, a number of people visit. Write down three people or groups who call.

3 Why are the children curious about the mattress?

4 Who do you think is the 'man of the appalling trade'?

5 What clue is there in line 12 that this poem is not based on Emily Dickinson's own life?

INTERPRETING THE TEXT

6 How does the narrator know that there has been a death?

7 What impression does the verb 'rustle' give of the neighbours?

8 What impression does the adverb 'stiffly' give of the minister?

9 What do you think the message of the poem is overall? Choose the statement you most agree with, or write your own different statement. Then write a sentence to explain your choice.

   a People always react in the same way to death.

   b People aren't really themselves after a death.

   c People are very formal following a death.

   d No one really cares about the family following a death.

10 What impression do you get of the narrator of the poem?

Hints
- Look at his attitude to what he sees.
- Think about whether he gets involved.
- Look at the way he describes people and events.

LANGUAGE AND STRUCTURE

1 Version A uses capital letters and punctuation very differently from Version B.

   a Read each version of the poem aloud. Do you read them differently because of the different punctuation? In what way?

   b How does the different punctuation change the meaning of the poem?

2 Look at the way the writer uses rhythm and rhyme in the poem.

   a Is it regular all the way through?

   b How do the rhythm and rhyme add to the effect of the poem? Do they make the subject seem more serious, or less?

3 How would you describe the tone of the poem (the writer's attitude to the subject)? Choose one of the words below, or give your own:

serious sombre fascinated horrified neutral curious

Explain your choice.

4 What clues are there in the language that the poem is set in a different period?

WRITING ACTIVITY

The poem describes the narrator's observations of people's reaction to a death in a small town. Rewrite the description to show how it would sound in prose rather than poetry – for example, as a diary entry or a description at the start of a novel. Use Standard English to describe the scene, and try to make your writing rich in detailed description.

What is gained or lost by presenting the material in this way? Write a paragraph comparing the effect of your work with that of the poem.

Twentieth-century poetry

Mid-term Break

Introduction

Seamus Heaney was born in 1939 and grew up in the countryside of Northern Ireland. He wrote about this in much of his early poetry, sometimes writing about his own family, and also reflecting on the political 'Troubles' of Ireland which have led to conflict and violence over hundreds of years.

This poem is a personal one and, like Emily Dickinson's poem on pages 122 to 123, it describes the writer's feelings following a death. The death is of the narrator's brother.

Glossary

knelling – *tolling (a death knell is a bell used at funerals)*

stanched – *the blood flow stopped*

Mid-term Break

I sat all morning in the college sick bay
Counting bells knelling classes to a close.
At two o'clock our neighbours drove me home.

In the porch I met my father crying –
He had always taken funerals in his stride –
And Big Jim Evans saying it was a hard blow.

The baby cooed and laughed and rocked the pram
When I came in, and I was embarrassed
By old men standing up to shake my hand

And tell me they were 'sorry for my trouble';
Whispers informed strangers I was the eldest,
Away at school, as my mother held my hand

In hers and coughed out angry tearless sighs.
At ten o'clock the ambulance arrived
With the corpse, stanched and bandaged by the nurses.

Next morning I went up into the room. Snowdrops
And candles soothed the bedside; I saw him
For the first time in six weeks. Paler now,

Wearing a poppy bruise on his left temple,
He lay in the four foot box as in his cot.
No gaudy scars, the bumper knocked him clear.

A four foot box, a foot for every year.

Seamus Heaney

UNDERSTANDING THE TEXT

1 Why does the narrator spend the morning in the sick bay? Is it because he is ill?

2 How do people first react when the narrator arrives home?

3 When he gets home, his house is full of sadness, except for the baby. What does the baby do?

4 How did his brother die?

5 How old was he when he died?

INTERPRETING THE TEXT

6 What do you learn about the narrator from the poem? How does he feel about what is going on?

7 In the room with his dead brother, there are snowdrops. Why do you think Seamus Heaney has included this detail about the type of flowers?

8 Look at these two statements:

a The narrator is very emotional.

b The narrator shows no emotion.

Write down which statement you most agree with, and say why.

LANGUAGE AND STRUCTURE

1 This text is set out in short lines like a poem, but are there any other language features that make it seem like poetry? Look for word patterns, rhythm and rhyme. Write a short paragraph saying what other evidence there is that this is a poem.

2 Look more closely at stanzas 1 and 2.

a How can you tell that this is set in the writer's childhood?

b How does the writer tell us that the section starting 'In the porch' happens a bit later than the first?

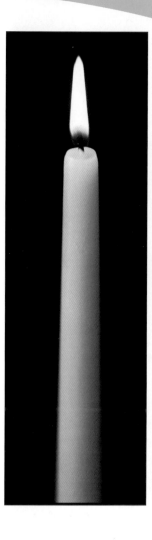

3 From stanzas 2 to 6, write down three words or phrases the writer uses as connectives to show that time has moved forward.

4 Look at the section from stanza 2 to the first line of stanza 5. Here, the writer uses quite long sentences. The poem then ends with much shorter sentences. What effect does this contrast in sentence types have? How does it add to the emotional impact of the poem?

5 The writer gives us information later in the poem that helps the reader to understand what happened earlier.

   a Find an example of this.

   b Explain why you think the writer uses this technique.

6 In pairs or a small group, discuss:

- how the writer creates a picture of his home and family
- how he builds emotion into the poem
- how the subject would have been presented differently if it was part of an autobiography or story, rather than a poem
- parts of the poem you particularly like or dislike.

WRITING ACTIVITY

1 After the discussion in question 6 above, write about your views of the poem. Remember to quote words and lines to support your argument. In particular, explain how the subject matter might have been presented differently if it was part of an autobiography or story, rather than a poem.

2 When you have finished, write an evaluation of your work on the poem. What have you done well, and which skills do you need to develop further for writing about poetry?

Unit 12 Extended writing

1 Look at the way Emily Dickinson writes in short, disjointed units of meaning, punctuated by dashes. Compare this with Seamus Heaney's more conversational style of storytelling to recount a memory from his childhood. Which style do you feel is more successful here, and why?

2 Choose a difficult or troubling experience from your life. Some examples are given below.

   ◆ a time you got into trouble

   ◆ the death of a pet

   ◆ suddenly being afraid that there was an intruder in your house

   ◆ being afraid of going to school

   ◆ learning to swim or ride a bike

   Try to write a short, powerful poem about the memory of this experience. Write about what happened and how it affected you. Spend time deciding on just the right words and images. Compress your language by cutting out any unnecessary words.

   You might try to use the style of Emily Dickinson or Seamus Heaney, or your own preferred style. Use rhyme and rhythm if appropriate.

   Your main aim should be to write something that captures and communicates the experience in an appropriate way.

3 Write a paragraph commenting upon your poem. What language decisions did you make? How did you change things after the first draft? Which parts of the poem do you think work especially well? Which are you less happy with?

Thriller writing

Introduction

When we read modern writers it can be easy to forget that they are often part of a tradition of writing. A novelist writing today may use techniques of characterization and plotting first used by a much earlier writer, such as Charles Dickens or Jane Austen.

The *Harry Potter* books, for example, have echoes of Charles Dickens's techniques in their memorable names and quirky characters. David Almond's novels, such as *Skellig* and *Kit's Wilderness*, have the clear, pure writing style of storytellers like Raymond Carver.

This unit is about tradition and influence, and the way the influence of one writer's work may emerge in the writing of a much later author. The main focus of the unit is on detective and mystery writing.

In the late nineteenth century, readers became intrigued by mystery stories. Charles Dickens had written an unfinished thriller called *The Mystery of Edwin Drood*. Other writers at the time created novels like *The Woman in White* by Wilkie Collins and *Dr Jekyll and Mr Hyde* by Robert Louis Stevenson.

It was also the period when Sherlock Holmes was invented by Sir Arthur Conan Doyle, and this led to a tradition of famous detectives in the writing of authors such as Georges Simenon, Dorothy L. Sayers, Agatha Christie, Raymond Chandler, Dashiell Hammett, Ruth Rendell, P.D. James and Patricia Cornwell.

In this unit we compare two thriller writers – one from the nineteenth century, the other from the twentieth: Edgar Allan Poe and Len Deighton.

On a Mission

Learning objectives

These are the objectives you will be studying:

- Word level: recognize layers of meaning

- Sentence level: integrate speech, reference and quotation into your writing; investigate ways English has changed over time

- Reading: compare the way ideas, values or emotions are presented; compare two writers from different times; explore the use of rhetorical devices; extend your understanding of literary heritage

- Writing: explore narrative techniques

Text A

Edgar Allan Poe is sometimes described as the creator of the detective story. He loved to create tales of horror and evil, as well as stories in which the reader had to try to guess – through the eyes of the expert detective – who the murderer might be. This was the beginning of the 'whodunnit'. The following extract from his short story 'The Tell Tale Heart' shows the mind of a murderer as he kills an old man by scaring him to death.

Glossary

death watches – *beetles that live in old wood, and make a ticking sound*

suppositions – *ideas*

waned – *wore out*

scantlings – *small wooden cross-beams*

The Tell Tale Heart

His room was as black as pitch with the thick darkness (for the shutters were close fastened through fear of robbers), and so I knew that he could not see the opening of the door, and I kept pushing it on steadily, steadily.

I had my head in, and was about to open the lantern, when my thumb slipped upon the tin fastening, and the old man sprang up in the bed, crying out, 'Who's there?'

I kept quite still and said nothing. For a whole hour I

did not move a muscle, and in the meantime I did not hear him lie down. He was still sitting up in the bed, listening; just as I have done night after night hearkening to the death watches in the wall.

Presently, I heard a slight groan, and I knew it was the groan of mortal terror. It was not a groan of pain or of grief – oh, no! It was the low stifled sound that arises from the bottom of the soul when overcharged with awe. I knew the sound well. Many a night, just at midnight, when all the world slept, it has welled up from my own bosom, deepening, with its dreadful echo, the terrors that distracted me. I say I knew it well. I knew what the old man felt, and pitied him although I chuckled at heart. I knew that he had been lying awake ever since the first slight noise when he had turned in the bed. His fears had been ever since growing upon him. He had been trying to fancy them causeless, but could not. He had been saying to himself, 'It is nothing but the wind in the chimney, it is only a mouse crossing the floor,' or, 'It is merely a cricket which has made a single chirp.' Yes, he had been trying to comfort himself with these suppositions; but he had found all in vain. ALL IN VAIN, because Death, in approaching him, had stalked with his black shadow before him and enveloped the victim. And it was the mournful influence of the unperceived shadow that caused him to feel, although he neither saw nor heard, to feel the presence of my head within the room.

When I had waited a long time very patiently without hearing him lie down, I resolved to open a little – a very, very little crevice in the lantern. So I opened it – you cannot imagine how stealthily, stealthily – until at length a single dim ray like the thread of the spider shot out from the crevice and fell upon the vulture eye.

It was open, wide, wide open, and I grew furious as I gazed upon it. I saw it with perfect distinctness – all a dull blue with a hideous veil over it that chilled the very marrow in my bones, but I could see nothing else of the old man's face or person, for I had directed the ray as if by instinct precisely upon the damned spot.

And now, have I not told you that what you mistake for madness is but over-acuteness of the senses? Now, I say, there came to my ears a low, dull, quick sound, such as a watch makes when enveloped in cotton. I knew that sound well too. It was the beating of the old man's heart. It increased my fury as the beating of a drum stimulates the soldier into courage.

But even yet I refrained and kept still. I scarcely breathed. I held the lantern motionless. I tried how steadily I could maintain the ray upon the eye. Meantime the hellish tattoo of the heart increased. It grew quicker and quicker, and louder and louder, every instant. The old man's terror must have been extreme! It grew louder, I say, louder every moment! –

do you mark me well? I have told you that I am nervous: so I am. And now at the dead hour of the night, amid the dreadful silence of that old house, so strange a noise as this excited me to uncontrollable terror. Yet, for some minutes longer I refrained and stood still. But the beating grew louder, louder! I thought the heart must burst. And now a new anxiety seized me – the sound would be heard by a neighbour! The old man's hour had come! With a loud yell, I threw open the lantern and leaped into the room. He shrieked once – once only. In an instant I dragged him to the floor, and pulled the heavy bed over him. I then smiled gaily, to find the deed so far done. But for many minutes the heart beat on with a muffled sound. This, however, did not vex me; it would not be heard through the wall. At length it ceased. The old man was dead. I removed the bed and examined the corpse. Yes, he was stone, stone dead. I placed my hand upon the heart and held it there many minutes. There was no pulsation. He was stone dead. His eye would trouble me no more.

If still you think me mad, you will think so no longer when I describe the wise precautions I took for the concealment of the body. The night waned, and I worked hastily, but in silence.

I took up three planks from the flooring of the chamber, and deposited all between the scantlings. I then replaced the boards so cleverly, so cunningly, that no human eye – not even his – could have detected anything wrong. There was nothing to wash out – no stain of any kind – no blood-spot whatever. I had been too wary for that.

Edgar Allan Poe

Text B

Len Deighton is a master of action novels, often set in a context of war or crime. Novels like this use a mix of plot, description and dialogue to keep up the pace. His writing uses many techniques for building suspense that can be traced back to writers such as Edgar Allan Poe. In this extract, an experienced soldier reflects upon a nervous young soldier.

Glossary

demented – *mad*

paraphernalia – *bits and pieces*

subordinates – *people he commands*

profiteer – *someone selling goods for large profits*

prevailed – *went on*

sedition – *rebellion*

CO – *commanding officer*

Mission Control: Hannibal One

All night I had been inside my headquarters, listening to the wind playing demented tunes upon the army badges, eagles and other paraphernalia that a publicity-conscious army commander had provided to mark the progress of our tiny expedition. I dressed myself in my heavy clothing before venturing outside. The wind blew with renewed violence as I emerged through the shelter's small flap. Each gust crooned a low warning that seemed to vibrate the whole planet before becoming the shrill complaining shriek that penetrated to the centre of my brain. It was a feat of willpower to think clearly. But I was the Mission Commander; unless I was able to think clearly, we might all die.

Others had been here, but only for a few hours at a time. We were the first soldiers to come, and now it looked as if we would be the first men to wage war here. It was a terrible place to fight a battle; a fatal place to lose it. It was a bleak, barren, metallic landscape like none other I had ever seen. I looked up through the clear air, and recognized the constellation of Pleiades, now setting. The neighbouring stars were growing dim. I remembered how as a child I had dreamed of travelling to them.

My second-in-command was an engineer. He was a balding veteran of many years. A fierce disciplinarian with his subordinates, even I was not immune from his sarcastic jeers about youth and inexperience. Perhaps that's why one of the southerners dealing out the rations that day decided to complain directly to me.

'This clothing isn't warm enough, sir. I didn't know it would be as cold as this.'

'You're wearing the same as the others,' I said. 'You'd be no use to the army in a cocoon.'

'It's such a poor-quality material the cold wind goes right through it,' he said, examining his white tunic with finger and thumb. 'A profiteer with an army contract and friends in the Senate doesn't have to worry about how cold we feel.'

'That's all, soldier,' I told him. I wasn't going to let these 'boots' think that the informality that prevailed on these missions extended to the privilege of sedition. 'You volunteered for the trip and your application was endorsed by your CO and agreed by me. Did we all make a mistake about you, soldier?'

'No, sir,' he yelled. 'It's just that where I come from in the south,' he smiled, because his accent made the

qualification unnecessary, 'we never knew temperatures like this.'

I looked at him. He was a weak-faced kid. He'd cut himself shaving, and a spider of dried blood crawled down his jawline. He was probably a good enough soldier left to do a soldier's job, but here he felt inadequate, and those were the ones who showed fear first.

'I'm not looking forward to the trip back, sir. And now the men say there will be fighting before we return.'

There had been mistakes and emergencies during the ascent. The boy needed reassurance. 'It's a routine mission. It was a thousand-to-one chance that they would have men up here, too.' It was a lie, but it seemed to do the trick for him.

'There's no doubt about them being here, then?'

'They're not local inhabitants, if that's what you mean,' I said rather brutally. I spoke too loud, I suppose. My second-in-command heard me and chortled. He looked forward to the fighting. For two decades he'd been in every war the army had fought and he knew that it was the quickest way to promotion. I kept my eyes on the youngster. 'Our mission is reconnaissance, but if they come into this area we will oppose their transit. If that means fighting, we fight.' I saw my Second nod. He turned towards us; he couldn't keep out of a conversation like this. He prodded the boy with enough force to make him wince.

'If you don't like it up here, go home,' he jeered.

Len Deighton

UNDERSTANDING THE TEXT

Text A

1 How can you tell from the start of the extract that the old man is nervous?

2 When the narrator hears the old man's groan, what does it remind him of?

3 When the narrator first notices the beating of the old man's heart, what effect does it have on him?

Text B

4 Look at the first paragraph. How can you tell that it is cold?

5 Why does the narrator feel a strong sense of responsibility?

6 Look at the second paragraph. Where do you think the story is set?

7 Why does the young soldier complain to the narrator rather than the second-in-command?

8 What clues are there that this is a very dangerous mission?

INTERPRETING THE TEXT

Text A

9 What impression do you get of the setting of the story? Where does it take place? What clues are there that it is an old story?

Text B

10 One reader might say: 'The story is set on a distant planet'. Another might say: 'The setting is on Earth, but the landscape is described in this way to show how harsh it is'. Which interpretation do you agree with? Using evidence from the text, explain why.

Comparison

11 What impression do you get of the two narrators? Choose two words or phrases (one for each narrator) that you think best sum them up:

tough heartless evil menacing mad soft at heart aggressive compassionate blunt nostalgic

Then write two sentences explaining your choice of words.

12 How can you tell that one story was written more recently than the other? What clues are there in the words and sentences? Write a brief paragraph explaining what you can tell about when they were written.

13 Study the similarities and differences in the two texts. Think about:

* the way the two narrators tell the stories

* the way the writers build suspense

* the disturbing mood of the texts.

Write two brief paragraphs explaining the similarities and differences. Then say which story you prefer and why.

LANGUAGE AND STRUCTURE

Text A

1 The writer uses personification in his story, like this:

Death, in approaching him, had stalked with his black shadow before him …

a What impression does this create of Death?

b Why do you think the writer uses this technique?

2 Sometimes the writer uses repetition to create an effect – for example:

But the beating grew louder, louder!

He might have said: 'But the beating grew louder and louder!' What effect do you think his use of repetition creates in this example?

Text B

3 Look at the writer's use of description. In the first sentence, what do you notice about the way he describes the wind?

4 Look at the way the young soldier speaks. How can you tell that:

a he is being polite

b he feels nervous about the mission?

5 Now look at the narrator's speech. How can you tell that he is:

a blunt in his speech

b sarcastic?

6 The writer includes speech within longer sentences that give more information about the speaker, or what he is thinking. Give an example of the writer integrating speech in this way.

WRITING ACTIVITY

Both writers help us to see into the minds of their narrators by using the first person ('I …' rather than 'he …').

How would the effect of the stories be different if they were written in the third person?

Choose one short extract from either story. Then rewrite it using the third person. Next, write a brief paragraph saying how you think the change of narrative voice changes the effect of the story.

Unit 13 Extended writing

Choose one of the writers below. They are all listed in the national curriculum for English because they are influential in the history of English literature.

Playwrights:

William Congreve, Oliver Goldsmith, Christopher Marlowe, Sean O'Casey, Harold Pinter, J.B. Priestley, Peter Shaffer, G.B. Shaw, R.B. Sheridan, Oscar Wilde

Fiction writers:

Jane Austen, Charlotte Brontë, Emily Brontë, John Bunyan, Wilkie Collins, Joseph Conrad, Daniel Defoe, Charles Dickens, Arthur Conan Doyle, George Eliot, Henry Fielding, Elizabeth Gaskell, Thomas Hardy, Henry James, Mary Shelley, Robert Louis Stevenson, Jonathan Swift, Anthony Trollope, H.G. Wells

Poets:

Matthew Arnold, William Blake, Emily Brontë, Robert Browning, Elizabeth Barrett Browning, Robert Burns, Lord Byron, Geoffrey Chaucer, John Clare, S.T. Coleridge, John Donne, John Dryden, Thomas Gray, George Herbert, Robert Herrick, Gerard Manley Hopkins, John Keats, Andrew Marvell, John Milton, Alexander Pope, Christina Rossetti, William Shakespeare (sonnets), Percy Bysshe Shelley, Edmund Spenser, Alfred Lord Tennyson, Henry Vaughan, William Wordsworth, Sir Thomas Wyatt

Assignment

Find out more about the writer you have chosen, and aim to produce a web page or poster about that author, which includes:

♦ biographical information (the writer's background)

♦ titles of some texts that she or he has written

♦ an extract from one text to show the writer's style

♦ a comment about why the writer was so influential.

Your aim is to make the information about the writer interesting to a general audience. Assume that your readers know nothing about the writer you have chosen. How will you make them want to start reading something by her or him?

On one side of A4 paper, sketch out how your web page or poster might look. It should combine:

◆ images

◆ text

◆ some interactive features (e.g. a quiz or competition).

Think about the style of writing you will use to interest your reader: how formal or informal will you be? Will you use a serious or humorous tone?

To do your research you could use:

◆ the school library

◆ CD-ROMs of literary material (e.g. guides to writers, images, etc.)

◆ the Internet.

Once you have finished your design, show it to other people in your group. Produce a class display on influential writers or – better still – create part of your school website devoted to this.

Influences on language and style

An Enemy of the People

> ## Learning objectives
>
> You will be studying the following objectives:
>
> - Word level: recognize layers of meaning
>
> - Sentence level: explore attitudes to language and identify characteristics of Standard English; investigate ways English has changed over time
>
> - Reading: comment on authors' perspectives; compare the way ideas, values or emotions are presented; explore the use of rhetorical devices; analyse scenes from plays; extend your understanding of literary heritage; explore the influence of cultural contexts and traditions
>
> - Writing: support your opinions of a text with evidence

Introduction

Shakespeare is certainly the best-known dramatist in English. But many other playwrights have also been influential in the history of world literature. This unit focuses on a Norwegian writer who has been called 'the father of modern drama'.

When Henrik Ibsen's plays first appeared in the late nineteenth century, audiences across Europe were shocked and scandalized. So much so, in fact, that Ibsen had to leave his home at one point.

Ibsen was controversial for two reasons. First, his plays dealt with issues that few writers had had the courage to address. For example, he showed women stifled by society and relationships, and treated as inferior. He showed what happened when they struggled to break free in a play called *A Doll's House*.

He was also controversial because of the way he used language. To audiences of the day, his language was shockingly ordinary. It was not literary language; it was like the language people spoke in their daily lives. This was a new concept – and it is hard to imagine now how upset people became when they heard major issues spoken about in everyday words.

In this way, Ibsen paved the way for twentieth-century realism – showing life as it is – and for soap operas.

This unit allows you to compare two very different versions of Ibsen's writing. One is a translation of his play by Michael Meyer – famous for his Ibsen translations. The second is by the well-known American dramatist Arthur Miller, who wrote his own translation of Ibsen's play.

The play, called *An Enemy of the People*, is about Dr Thomas Stockmann, who learns that the water in his town's water supply is polluted. He knows he has to warn the people. But he quickly finds that this is less easy than he thinks – local politicians and the media are terrified of the effect of bad publicity. So they fight to stop him from making the truth known.

Start by reading the opening from Michael Meyer's translation of the play. Then compare it with Arthur Miller's. This extract takes place in Dr Stockmann's home and features his relatives, although he doesn't appear until later in the play.

Read the play aloud in a small group. For each script you will need readers for the following characters:

- Mrs Thomas Stockmann
- Mayor (Peter Stockmann)
- Morten Kiil (only in Text B)
- Billing
- Hovstad

Text A

> *Evening in DR STOCKMANN'S living-room. It is humbly but neatly furnished and decorated. In the wall to the right are two doors, of which the further leads out to the hall and the nearer to the DOCTOR'S study. In the opposite wall, facing the hall door, is a door that leads to the other rooms occupied by the family. In the middle of this wall stands a tiled stove; further downstage is a sofa with a mirror above it. In front of the sofa is an oval table*

with a cloth on it. Upon this table stands a lighted lamp with a shade. Upstage, an open door to the dining-room in which can be seen a table laid for the evening meal, with a lamp on it.

At this table BILLING is seated, a napkin tucked beneath his chin. MRS STOCKMANN is standing by the table, offering him a plate with a large joint of beef on it. The other places around the table are empty, and the table is in the disorder of a meal that has been finished.

MRS STOCKMANN: There, Mr Billing! But if you will come an hour late, you'll have to put up with cold.

BILLING (*eating*): Oh, but this is capital. Absolutely capital!

MRS STOCKMANN: Well you know how punctually my husband always likes to eat –

BILLING: It doesn't bother me. I enjoy eating alone, without having to talk to anyone.

MRS STOCKMANN: Oh. Well, as long as you're enjoying it, that's – (*Listens towards the hall.*) Ah, this must be Mr Hovstad.

BILLING: Very likely.

MAYOR PETER STOCKMANN enters wearing an overcoat and his official hat and carrying a stick.

MAYOR: Good evening to you, my dear sister-in-law.

MRS STOCKMANN (*goes into the living-room*): Why, good evening! Fancy seeing you here! How nice of you to come and call on us!

MAYOR: I just happened to be passing so – (*Glances towards the dining-room.*) But I hear you have company.

MRS STOCKMANN (*a little embarrassed*): Oh, no, no, that's no one. (*Quickly.*) Won't you have something too?

MAYOR: I? No, thank you! Good heavens, a cooked meal at night! My digestion would never stand that!

MRS STOCKMANN: Oh, but surely just for once –

MAYOR: No, no! It's very kind of you, but I'll stick to my tea and sandwiches. It's healthier in the long run; and a little less expensive.

MRS STOCKMANN (*smiles*): You speak as though Thomas and I were spend-thrifts!

MAYOR: Not you, my dear sister-in-law. Such a thought was far from my mind. (*Points towards the DOCTOR'S study.*) Isn't he at home?

MRS STOCKMANN: No, he's gone for a little walk with the boys.

MAYOR: I wonder if that's wise so soon after a meal? (*Listens.*) Ah, this must be he.

MRS STOCKMANN: No, I don't think it can be, yet. (*A knock on the door.*) Come in!

HOVSTAD, the editor of the local newspaper, enters from the hall.

HOVSTAD: Yes. Please excuse me, I was detained down at the printer's. Good evening, Your Worship.

MAYOR (*greets him somewhat stiffly*): Good evening. I suppose you are here on business?

Trans. Michael Meyer

Text B

It is evening. Dr Stockmann's living room is simply but cheerfully furnished. A doorway, upstage right, leads into the entrance hall, which extends from the front door to the dining room, running unseen behind the living room. At the left is another door, which leads to the Doctor's study and other rooms. In the upstage left corner is a stove. Toward the left foreground is a sofa with a table behind it. In the right foreground are two chairs, a small table between them, on which stand a lamp and a bowl of apples. At the back, to the left, an open doorway leads to the dining room, part of which is seen. The windows are in the right wall, a bench in front of them.

As the curtain rises, Billing and Morten Kiil are eating in the dining room. Billing is junior editor of the People's Daily Messenger. *Kiil is a slovenly old man who is feeding himself in a great hurry. He gulps his last bite and comes into the living room, where he puts on his coat and ratty fur hat. Billing comes in to help him.*

BILLING: You sure eat fast, Mr Kiil. (*Billing is an enthusiast to the point of foolishness.*)

KIIL: Eating don't get you anywhere, boy. Tell my daughter I went home.

Kiil starts across to the front door. Billing returns to his food in the dining room. Kiil halts at the bowl of apples; he takes one, tastes it, likes it, takes another and puts it in his pocket, then continues on toward the door. Again he stops, returns, and takes another apple for his pocket. Then he sees a tobacco can on the table. He covers his action from Billing's possible glance, opens the can, smells it, pours some into his side pocket. He is just closing the can when Catherine Stockmann enters from the dining room.

MRS STOCKMANN: Father! You're not going, are you?

KIIL: Got business to tend to.

MRS STOCKMANN: Oh, you're only going back to your room and you know it. Stay! Mr Billing's here, and Hovstad's coming. It'll be interesting for you.

KIIL: Got all kinds of business. The only reason I came over was the butcher told me you bought roast beef today. Very tasty, dear.

MRS STOCKMANN: Why don't you wait for Tom? He only went for a little walk.

KIIL (*taking out his pipe*): You think he'd mind if I filled my pipe?

MRS STOCKMANN: No, go ahead. And here – take some apples. You should always have fruit in your room.

KIIL: No, no, wouldn't think of it.

The doorbell rings.

MRS STOCKMANN: That must be Hovstad. (*She goes to the door and opens it.*)

Peter Stockmann, the Mayor, enters. He is a bachelor, nearing sixty. He has always been one of those men who make it their life work to stand in the centre of the ship to keep it from overturning. He probably envies the family life and warmth of this house, but when he comes he never wants to admit he came and often sits with his coat on.

MRS STOCKMANN: Peter! Well, this is a surprise!

PETER STOCKMANN: I was passing by … (*He sees Kiil and smiles, amused.*) Mr Kiil!

KIIL (*sarcastically*): Your Honor! (*He bites into his apple and exits.*)

MRS STOCKMANN: You mustn't mind him, Peter, he's getting terribly old. Would you like a bite to eat?

PETER STOCKMANN: No, no thanks. (*He sees Billing now, and Billing nods to him from the dining room.*)

MRS STOCKMANN (*embarrassed*): He just happened to drop in.

PETER STOCKMANN: That's all right. I can't take hot food in the evening. Not with my stomach.

MRS STOCKMANN: Can't I ever get you to eat anything in this house?

PETER STOCKMANN: Bless you, I stick to my tea and toast. Much healthier and more economical.

MRS STOCKMANN (*smiling*): You sound as though Tom and I throw money out the window.

PETER STOCKMANN: Not you, Catherine. He wouldn't be home, would he?

MRS STOCKMANN: He went for a little walk with the boys.

PETER STOCKMANN: You don't think that's dangerous, right after dinner? (*There is a loud knocking on the front door.*) That sounds like my brother.

MRS STOCKMANN: I doubt it, so soon. Come in, please.

Hovstad enters. He is in his early thirties, a graduate of the peasantry struggling with a terrible conflict. For while he hates authority and wealth, he cannot bring himself to cast off a certain desire to partake of them. Perhaps he is dangerous because he wants more than anything to belong, and in a radical that is a withering wish, not easily to be borne.

MRS STOCKMANN: Mr Hovstad –

HOVSTAD: Sorry I'm late. I was held up at the printing shop.*(Surprised)* Good evening, Your Honor.

PETER STOCKMANN (*rather stiffly*): Hovstad. On business, no doubt.

Trans. Arthur Miller

UNDERSTANDING THE TEXT

Text A

1 Write down one detail from the opening stage directions that tells you the play is set in the past.

2 Explain in your own words what the writer means by 'the table is in the disorder of a meal that has been finished'.

3 Why does Mr Billing enjoy eating alone?

Text B

4 Write down two ways in which the setting in this version of the play is different from Text A.

5 What impression do you get from the description 'a ratty fur hat'?

6 How can you tell that Peter Stockmann is a fussy person?

INTERPRETING THE TEXT

7 What clues can you find in the language that:

   a Text A translates a text written a long time ago?

   b Text B is by an American writer?

8 Does the character of Peter Stockmann seem exactly the same in both texts, or do the two writers present him slightly differently? Support your response with examples.

9 Look at this comment on the two versions of the play:

Text A is less descriptive. It gives us the words that characters say, but little else. The stage directions in Text B help us much more to visualize the scene.

Do you agree with this comment? Say why or why not.

10 Henrik Ibsen is described as a very modern writer because of the way he presents themes and characters, and his use of language. Write a paragraph giving your response to these two extracts.

   ◆ In what ways does he seem like a modern writer to you?

   ◆ Which of the two translations do you prefer and why?

LANGUAGE AND STRUCTURE

Text A

1 Look at the stage directions. Why do you think these are written in the present rather than the past tense?

2 In his first speech, Mr Billing says '… this is capital. Absolutely capital!' This word was used in the past to describe something that was really good. Think of a word someone might use today in an informal situation.

3 What do we learn about Mrs Stockmann's character from this scene? Write down three things we are shown about her.

Text B

4 This version uses some non-standard language – for example:

Eating don't get you anywhere, boy.

  a How would this be expressed in Standard English?

  b Why do you think the translator uses a non-standard form like this?

  c Why might plays use non-Standard English more than some other types of text?

5 Look at the way Peter Stockmann is described in this text:

He has always been one of those men who make it their life work to stand in the centre of the ship to keep it from overturning.

  a What do you think the writer means by this metaphor?

  b Why do you think he uses a metaphorical phrase rather than a literal one?

6 This scene is structured around the entrances of characters.

  a Write down the order in which the characters appear onstage.

  b Does anyone exit the stage in this scene?

WRITING ACTIVITY

Plays rely on dialogue to tell their stories. Henrik Ibsen is famous for creating a new, realistic kind of dialogue.

a Choose one example from each text of dialogue that feels very authentic (just like real life).

Write each example down, then explain why it seems so realistic. Be as specific as you can about the words and phrases in your chosen pieces.

b Find one example from *either* of the texts where you think the dialogue seems less realistic. Write it down and explain why.

Extended writing

Henrik Ibsen is sometimes described as the writer who made soap opera possible.

In pairs or a small group, do a research project into soap operas. This will test your teamwork and problem-solving skills.

Try to answer this question:

Which soap opera uses language in the most realistic way?

Your task is to:

◆ compare two or more soap operas (e.g. *EastEnders* and *Coronation Street*)

◆ study the way they use language

◆ write a brief report giving your results, or make a presentation to your class.

First you should think about the following questions:

◆ What makes dialogue realistic?

◆ What features of everyday speech will you be looking for?

To help with these questions, you could listen to a conversation between two people in real life and note the features of language they use (e.g. repetition, not completing sentences, fillers like *er* and *um*, overlapping speech, no clear structure). Make a checklist of features.

Use this checklist when you listen to a one- or two-minute extract from two different soap operas. Ideally, you need to record these so that you can replay them for better analysis.

Once you have some results, think about how you will write them down and present your report. Remember that you are aiming to present information as clearly as possible to your audience. What layout features might help (e.g. tables, charts, bullet points)?

Poetic fable

The Tiger and the Deer

Learning objectives

You will be studying the following objectives:

- Word level: recognize layers of meaning
- Reading: comment on authors' perspectives in texts from different cultures; explore the use of rhetorical devices; explore the influence of cultural contexts and traditions
- Writing: explore narrative techniques

Introduction

Literature in English has been influenced by texts from all kinds of cultures. Greek myths, for example, have played a powerful part in storytelling. Irish short stories, American drama, West Indian poetry and European plays have all shaped the way English literature has developed.

First, this unit takes a poem from India and explores how far it feels like the kind of fable or legend we expect from early English literature.

Start by looking at the title and making some predictions – not just on what the poem will be about, but also the kind of poem it will be. Does the title remind you of other texts, in particular stories from your childhood?

Read the poem and look at the way the writer uses poetic language to unfold a story.

Glossary

lest – *in case*

THE TIGER AND THE DEER

Brilliant, crouching, slouching, what crept through the green heart of the forest,
Gleaming eyes and mighty chest and soft soundless paws of grandeur and murder?
The wind slipped through the leaves as if afraid lest its voice and the noise of its steps disturb the pitiless Splendour,
Hardly daring to breathe. But the great beast crouched and crept, and crept and crouched a last time, noiseless, fatal,
Till suddenly death leaped on the beautiful wild deer as it drank
Unsuspecting from the great pool in the forest's coolness and shadow,
And it fell and, torn, died remembering its mate left sole in the deep woodland, –
Destroyed, the mild harmless beauty by the strong cruel beauty in Nature.
But the day may yet come when the tiger crouches and leaps no more in the dangerous heart of the forest,
As the mammoth shakes no more the plains of Asia;
Still then shall the beautiful wild deer drink from the coolness of great pools in the leaves' shadow.
The mighty perish in their might;
The slain survive the slayer.

Aurobindo Ghose

UNDERSTANDING THE TEXT

1 The poem describes two creatures. Find a word or phrase which is used to describe the tiger and another word or phrase which describes the deer.

2 What happens to the deer?

3 The writer mentions the 'heart of the forest' twice. Which two adjectives are used to describe it?

4 How would you sum up what happens in the poem in one sentence?

INTERPRETING THE TEXT

5 How does the writer show the power and danger of the tiger?

6 Why does the writer compare the tiger with the mammoth?

7 The poem is like a fable or a parable – a story with a message. What message do you think the poem is offering?

8 What is the writer's attitude to the two creatures: does he admire one more than the other, admire both equally, or remain neutral? Explain your answer.

LANGUAGE AND STRUCTURE

1 Look at the first four lines of the poem. How does the writer use patterns of words to show:

a the movement of the tiger

b the silence?

2 The writer uses personification to describe the wind (treats it as if it is human). What does he show the wind to be like?

3 Find an example of the way the writer uses repetition of sounds or structures to create his effects. Write down the example, and then write a sentence describing how it works.

4 Part of the poem is written in the past tense. Part of it is written in the future tense. Find the line where the poem shifts to the future tense. Why do you think the writer does this?

WRITING ACTIVITY

How could the poem be retold in prose as a story for young children? Write a short story called 'The Tiger and the Deer' based on the poem, aimed at children aged five to eight.

Think about the narrative techniques you will use. Instead of using third-person narration, you could write from the point of view of the tiger, of the deer, or switch between both (multiple narration).

Nostalgic poem
My Moccasins Have Not Walked

Introduction

The following poem was written by Duke Redbird, a native American painter, poet, actor, political activist and film-maker, who was born on the Saugeen Reserve on the Bruce Peninsula in Ontario.

Redbird had a dramatic childhood. He was the youngest of six children. When his mother died trying to save her children from a fire that destroyed their home, Redbird, who was nine months old, was sent to live with a white foster family. At the age of 11, when his foster father died, he began a journey from foster home to foster home, often running away to try to find his birth father and family. There followed a rough period in street gangs and doing odd jobs. Later he became a poet, lecturer and film-maker.

Glossary

moccasins – *a soft leather shoe traditionally worn by some native American peoples*

beheld – *seen*

adorned – *decorated*

My Moccasins have not walked

My Moccasins have not walked
Among the giant forest trees
My leggings have not brushed
Against the fern and berry bush
My medicine pouch has not been filled
With roots and herbs and sweetgrass
My hands have not fondled the speckled fawn

My eyes have not beheld
The golden rainbow of the north
My hair has not been adorned with the eagle feather
Yet
My dreams are dreams of these
My heart is one with them
The scent of them caresses my soul

Duke Redbird

UNDERSTANDING THE TEXT

1 Name three objects or items of clothing that show the writer is a native American.

2 What does the writer mean when he says he has not 'fondled the speckled fawn'?

3 What do you think the writer means in the last line of the poem?

INTERPRETING THE TEXT

4 How can you tell that the writer is referring to a different culture from the one he has been brought up in?

5 The writer uses the same formula at the start of many sentences: 'My Moccasins …', 'My leggings …', 'My medicine pouch …'. Why do you think he does this rather than using the first person pronoun, *I*?

6 Decide which of the following words you would use to describe the tone of the poem:

> sad moody regretful proud mystical cheerful nostalgic hopeful

Write a sentence to explain your choice.

7 What impression do you get of the narrator of the poem?

LANGUAGE AND STRUCTURE

1 Read this comment from a reader:

> *This poem is in two sections. One part describes what the writer has not experienced. The other part describes how he wishes he had. The two parts are linked by a key word.*

a Do you agree with the reader's description of the poem?

b Which key word links the two sections?

2 The poem is written as if it is being spoken aloud by someone. It contains no punctuation at all. Why do you think the writer chose not to use punctuation?

3 The first section of the poem contains concrete nouns – things that you can actually see or touch, such as 'moccasins', 'roots', 'herbs' and so on. At the end of the poem the nouns are more abstract – for example, 'dreams', 'heart', 'soul'. Why do you think the vocabulary changes in this way?

4 Look again at the last line of the poem. It could be rewritten like this:

> the **smell** of them **strokes** my soul

How do these two changes of vocabulary change the effect of the writing?

5 The poem contains a range of different types of words. Look at the list below and see if you can find examples of:

a words describing nature

b adjectives about size or shape or appearance

c vocabulary that feels archaic (old-fashioned)

d words placed side-by-side for alliteration (repetition of the starting sounds)

WRITING ACTIVITY

What do you think of Duke Redbird's poem? What do you like or dislike about it? What is its message? How does the writer use language to create a mood and to tell his story? Write two paragraphs giving your response.

In the first paragraph:

- describe what you have learned about the poem
- describe its structure
- say something about the writer's use of vocabulary
- comment on the lack of punctuation
- describe what you think the poem is saying
- do not give your opinion at this stage, so avoid saying 'I' and 'me'.

In the second paragraph:

- give your opinion
- say what you like about the poem
- mention anything you don't understand
- comment on anything you dislike
- mention any other texts it reminds you of
- say what you think of the poem overall.

Unit 15 Extended writing

In your English lessons you will be able to read drama, fiction and poetry by major writers from different cultures and traditions.

Here are some of the examples given in the national curriculum:

Drama: Athol Fugard, Arthur Miller, Wole Soyinka, Tennessee Williams

Fiction: Chinua Achebe, Maya Angelou, Willa Cather, Anita Desai, Nadine Gordimer, Ernest Hemingway, H.H. Richardson, Doris Lessing, R.K. Narayan, John Steinbeck, Ngugi wa Thiong'o

Poetry: E.K. Brathwaite, Emily Dickinson, Robert Frost, Robert Lowell, Les Murray, Rabindranath Tagore, Derek Walcott

Choose one of these writers – perhaps one you know nothing about. Working on your own or in a pair, find out more about the writer. Research some details about the writer's background, and what she or he has written.

When you have collected your information, think about how you can present it most effectively to others in your class. Perhaps you can create a poster or display. Include the following:

- ◆ information on the writer's background
- ◆ titles of some texts by the writer
- ◆ an extract from a text to show the writer's style
- ◆ a comment on the way the writer reflects his or her culture.

Unit 10 Narrative and structure

Look back at some of the narrative writing you have produced in the past year. Review how your narrative writing is developing by drawing up a grid, starting like the one below.

Narrative writing review	
Features that have improved	**Features that need developing**

List the following features in the appropriate columns:

◆ strong opening

◆ interesting story structure

◆ unexpected ending

◆ dialogue

◆ vivid descriptive language

◆ interesting narrative devices (e.g. multiple narration)

Unit 11 Non-fiction texts

1 Think about how you performed during the interview for the speaking and listening assignment on page 120. Ask for some feedback from your interview partner.

2 Look through the list of skills below and give yourself a 1 to 5 rating for each. A rating of level 1 means 'needs more work'. A rating of level 5 means 'very good'.

Speaking and listening skill	Rating 1, 2, 3, 4, or 5
Plan your questions	
Ask open questions (i.e. not questions that just have yes/no answers)	
Keep the interview going	
Think on your feet instead of just relying on notes	
Stay in role	
Speak loudly and clearly enough	

Unit 12 Poetic forms and styles

1 Working with a partner, draw two spider diagrams to note what you have learned about the writing of Emily Dickinson and Seamus Heaney. You might include:

- what you have learned about them as poets
- what you have learned about their subject matter, style and use of language
- what you liked or disliked about their work
- words or phrases that you found unusual or memorable.

2 How have your skills in reading and responding to poetry developed? With a partner, discuss the skills you need to read and respond to poetry. (You might find it helpful to think about how you answered the questions about the poems on pages 124 to 125 and 127 to 129.) Then write a paragraph using these prompts:

> When I used to read poetry I …
> When I read these poems I …
> My response to poetry now is …

Unit 13 Writers from different times

In this unit you compared extracts from two thrillers. Think carefully about how your reading skills are developing.

Use the rating scale * (low) to ***** (high) to show how your confidence levels are improving. Rate your confidence in each of these skill areas:

1 I can read a long extract without being distracted.
2 I can usually follow what is happening.
3 I can find something to say about the story.
4 I can find something to say about the characters.
5 I can comment on the author's style and language.
6 I can support my opinion with examples.
7 I can use quotations built into my own sentences.
8 I can say why a text seems to have been written in another time.

Unit 14 Drama scripts

1 Look at the research project you produced for the extended writing task (page 150). Evaluate your performance in the areas listed in the grid below.

Attitude towards the task	Good	Not bad	Could be better
Organizing the stages of the task	Good	Not bad	Could be better
Working with others	Good	Not bad	Could be better
Comparing the soap operas	Good	Not bad	Could be better
Studying language	Good	Not bad	Could be better

2 Evaluate what you produced – whether a written report or presentation. List its strengths and weaknesses in a grid, like the one started below.

3 List the three main areas you need to develop for next time you work on a project like this.

Strengths	Weaknesses

Unit 15 Cultural context

Work with a partner to evaluate the poster or display you produced for the extended writing task on page 157.

1 Give feedback on your partner's work. Make comments about:

   ♦ how informative the display is (what did you learn?)

   ♦ how interesting it is (what has your partner done to catch your attention?)

   ♦ how well presented it is (what is the overall design like?).

Make sure your comments are precise. Try not to use words such as 'good' or 'okay'. Look at the vocabulary box below so that your feedback is sharper.

Vocabulary box: words that may prove useful
How informative: informative, interesting, fascinating, detailed, historical, biographical
How interesting: lively, entertaining, interactive, questioning, innovative, unusual
How well presented: colourful, vivid, eye-catching, structure, text, images, headings

2 Think carefully about your own work. How would you improve each area if you were doing a similar task again?